The Entrepreneur's Guide Series

DEVELOPING A COMPANY POLICY MANUAL

That Both You & Your Employees Can Live With

Michael Reaves

PROBUS PUBLISHING COMPANY
Chicago, Illinois
Cambridge, England

ISBN 1-55738-258-1

Printed in the United States of America

IPC

1 2 3 4 5 6 7 8 9 0

Dedication

I can never sufficiently express my gratitude of the support I received while writing this book, even that which was forced on me. I am thankful for all the friends who saw me go loudly nuts and stuck around to see the ending.

Paul Thompson, a feistiest entrepreneur and breeder of businesses. Over 30 firms have been born under his supervision.

Robert Kiyosaki, my sensi, a peaceful warrior.

D.C. Cordoba, citizen of the world, native of Chile, fiercely in love with the "dance of life."

David Oreck, a mind diamond sharp, an example for American business.

And, finally to

Barbara Forsythe, especially this lady, my friend, my teacher and mentor who painstakingly reviews every word I write. Barbara, thank you from the graduating "Class of Life."

Contents

Preface

This book is the result of many hours of research and accumulated years of experience. It was initially intended to be a policy handbook for a small chain of retail stores whose managers were all members of one family. This chain was doing poorly, for the reason that within each store, employees followed the dictates of their manager in dealing with customers. Sometimes the results were good; other times, they were disastrous. Moreover, whenever a manager took a vacation or went on a business trip, employees were left to their own devices. The managing family desperately needed a set of policies that governed the entire chain of stores in a uniform manner.

To allow each family member an equal say in establishing policies, this book was designed with several options for each topic. Each manager was urged to rewrite every topic designated as applicable, and a group consensus was solicited. As a result, the chain now has a uniform set of policies that have been approved by all its managers and readily accepted by its employees.

In its present form, this book presents an expanded list of topics and options for consideration by the management of any company. Pick an option from each topic and stick to it, even if consensus cannot be reached. Having a policy, even one that is less than perfect, is better than not having one.

Acknowledgments

There is no way that this book could have been written without the assistance of many helpful, cooperative people. Some compiled data, others did research and some gave bits of advice that only a sage could give. There were even those who gave encouragement, they most of all. Because of the amount of help across such a broad range of topics, I cannot thank them enough.

As a reader you could do well to remember them. They will influence many of our country's attitudes and policies for the future of business as it is ever evolving.

The City of Dallas Public Library Staff—especially the Renner Branch staff
The University of Texas in Austin Library Staff
The University of Texas in Austin—Bureau of Business Research
U.S. Department of Labor
U.S. Department of Health and Human Resources
Texas Department of Labor and Standards
Pension Benefit Guaranty Corporation

Texas State Board of Insurance
The American Association of Nurserymen
Federal Labor Relations Authority
U.S. Equal Employment Opportunity Commission
The Texas Employment Commission
U.S. Office of Personnel Management

CHAPTER 1

POLICY CONSIDERATIONS

The Purpose of Policy

The primary purpose of policies is to further the objectives of the company. Thus, you will want to avoid enacting ill-considered policies that could harm the company. Or, if you must establish a policy that could have negative side effects, then you will want to minimize the potential for harm. In formulating a policy statement, you usually express a known objective and determine how to accomplish that objective in a manner consistent with the company philosophy and conductive to active participation and acceptance from employees.

Another purpose of policies is to deter temporary problems becoming permanent. For example, advance planning for quick response to the unexpected or out-of-the ordinary event can prevent detrimental long-term effects to the company and its goals.

Some policies act as protection to the company by stating a desire to comply with laws, and others provide for protection by gaining the acceptance of employees to act in the best interest of the company as a component of their employment. Some protect the company by limiting risks an employee might undertake, during a highly charged incident.

The bottom line in directing policies is to foster the growth of the company's goals.

The Reasons For Policy

Many sound business reasons support having a written policy of your company's views and attitudes. Reasons range from providing legal protection to the company and its employees, to fostering a more productive work environment. The primary value of a written policy manual, however, is ensuring uniformity in response to a particular set of important subjects.

This uniformity should allow all personnel to know that a fair and equitable set of standards governs major aspects of their work lives. If your policies are well laid out, your customers will sense this through their interaction with your company. The fostering of good feelings, derived from the knowledge of being treated fairly and the respect of peers is the best way to promote company.

Successful companies, as a rule of thumb, are started by individuals with a strong set of attitudes about how things should be done. These people usually have no policy manual when they start but as their companies progress and employees are added, it becomes apparent that some uniformity of the original essence of the company be reinforced and made a part of every employee's responsibility to the company.

For example, the way an individual with technical training and background would handle a particular matter probably differs from how a cashier might handle the same situation. A written policy provides for uniform response by all personnel. In addition, as with many other areas of our daily lives company policy is affected by local, state, and federal laws designed to curb abuses. Almost every businessman is familiar with federal guidelines concerning age discrimination and with child labor laws, and company policy must meet those standards.

What Policies are Needed

When deciding what policies your firm needs, you might list those matters that you see as areas that possibly need addressing. Then ask your key members of management to do the same and seek participation from other employees as well. This procedure produces a basis of where to start, especially as you may expect to see the same set of topics appear several times. Often managers have similar concerns and perceive company needs in similar ways. Should you not feel that all members will cooperate try to get each one to agree to follow the Rules of Communication in Appendix E.

After you have found areas of general concern, then find those areas of specific interest to the well-being and growth of the goals that the company has established whether, written or implied.

What you are doing is setting up the different layers of policy. They may overlap, yet they must continue to be uniform and not conflict with each other. These policies may start with very broad concepts, such as the agreement to agree to specific policies concerning how departments will cooperate and interact with each other.

Arrange the policies in such a manner that, even though overlap does occur, their importance to the goals of the company and each other is reflected; that is, the most important policy is not superseded by a lesser policy. For example departmental needs should not be placed above the company's. In short, set some form of ranking.

After you have evaluated the needs, established their order of importance, and considered the effects upon personnel, then you should consider how to allow feedback from all levels. This information flow allows you to check the pulse of your company. Upper level management can and occasionally does lose the ability to perceive what line managers need. And since needs continually change, it is vital to the health of the company that you put in place some form of cross communication and feedback. A structure that allows adjustment and fine tuning on a regular basis could be the difference between becoming stagnant and meeting company needs now and in the future.

The bottom line concerning any policy matter is that this must be an executive-level decision, however feedback from line managers is necessary for highest group acceptance. After all, these are the people who actually implement policies; and if anyone is going to find where weakness are, it will be the people who use them.

Who Decides Policy

Although feedback is essential when establishing needs, the only people qualified to decide policy are those who are charged with setting the goals of the organization and seeing to it those goals are met, whether the original founding body or current management. Neither a subordinate nor a consultant is better qualified; and the methods that you instinctively know to be best for your company are not the same as policies designed by someone else.

Only under proper circumstances can a consultant assume part of the load from management. Despite the consultant's specialized experience, his or her efforts to work through the process of establishing policies for another company or organization require close contact with and communication from management. The chance for success in working with a consultant is in direct ratio to the amount of communication between management and the consultant.

If you decide to use the services of a consultant, the best guideline is to follow your intuition. If at any point you feel uncomfortable with the consultant's recommendations and cannot determine why you feel uneasy, terminate the relationship.

Case in point: I was asked to help in producing a program of changes for a firm that had a young dynamic president. His views were very strong, and he did not take easily to the idea of having someone question how or why he did things. After a week, it became apparent that we were not accomplishing the objective of capturing the essence that embodied the firm's way of operating, its philosophy, and that the only items he could agree to were those mandated by law.

As I look back on this, it is now apparent that many indicators were shouting to us both, but we did not recognize them for what they were.

The president was very conscious of the feeling that mistakes were not tolerated, especially if he were involved in a project. He did not feel that it was worth spending time or money on a project that he already knew all about. In addition he was somewhat resentful and fearful that written policy might place restrictions on him.

In my own case, I did not foresee that even though the twelve people in the company were all responsible individuals, that's exactly what they were—individuals, and all resented the idea of anyone setting guidelines they had agreed to follow. No single person there was sufficiently trusted or deemed qualified by the other members to set the policies of the firm. Thus they had brought in a consultant. I should have recognized this and not attempted to produce a policy that covered all of the individuals. Such an endeavor was as impossible as trying to produce a policy for twelve competing companies in one document.

This book is the result of hours of research and the accumulation of years of experience. I believe your company can benefit from the implementation of the contents. With proper fore-thought and implementation of this book, your firm will see the positive activities written policies permit.

When conceived, this book focused on one group of companies in a very narrow field. Within this small chain of identically named retail stores, the managers were all family members, each at a different store. These businessmen were struggling because the individual store managers and their employees had diverse opinions about how things should be done, some with good and others with disastrous results. Within each store, employees reflected the attitude of their own manager and passed that attitude on, to their customers. Thus each store developed different set of customer attitudes and expectations. To confuse the customers' perceptions further, continuity evaporated whenever one of the managers took a vacation or made a business trip. Each store was different even though the name was the same. As you can imagine, their customers had a different experience each time he ventured into one of these establishments. They desperately needed clear policies that governed the entire chain of stores in a uniform manner.

To allow each family member an equal say in establishing policies, this book was designed with options for each topic. Then each manager was urged each to rewrite every topic designated as applicable. Finally, a group consensus was required of all parties. As a result, their policies now have the approval of all presented in a uniform and fair manner. They know how each of the others is acting, and are pleased with how easily their employees accepted this "new" company image.

Following this initial experience and that gained with guiding other firms in developing company policies, you are presented with an expanded the list of topics and options to allow for flexibility of application to a broad spectrum of companies.

In summation, I can't over emphasize: if you cannot decide who is qualified to make policy, do it yourself. However, do not be put off by these cautions. Any policy is better than no policy—even bad policy! At least everyone is working toward a uniform goal and not making up policy individually as they go along.

CHAPTER 2

PRACTICABLE APPLICATION OF THIS BOOK

How To Use This Guide

A company policy manual is a most important "tool" for you and your employees. It serves as the "game plan" that helps all members of the organizational team work with the same set of rules and objectives, guided by the same company philosophy.

Developing a Company Policy Manual lists various subjects that deserve attention in your policy manual. Choose the option under each subject that best describes your own practices. If your choice is not included under any subject, consider revising one of the options to fit your situation.

Specialized Industries

A few fields of business are so regulated that only highly skilled and experienced professionals are capable of keeping up with developments and maintaining industry standards. The complexity involved is such that whole departments are devoted to maintaining the uniformity of the organization's policies.

For example, consider the banking industry. So many rules and regulations involve the banking industry that entire companies have evolved just to service single, highly specialized facets of the industry's needs. And, outside firms have stepped in to assist banks in the construction of the specialized policies they must have.

After an interview with the head of one bank, we stepped down the hall to examine the library, a room devoted to this banks policies and procedures. I was stunned to learn that it was a normal course of events for examiners to read the banks vast array of manuals and then to critique them in writing by offering "strongly suggested" areas that need attention.

In looking over some of the "policy" manuals, I could not say that I recognized them as such. The amount of detail was so in depth that they appeared to be very involved procedural devices. It was explained that the tremendous amount of detail was required by the examiners so that they would have a method of judging the compliance of the bank to equal lending practices.

Other examples in this group include airlines, trains, trucking and the government itself. This book is not intended to handle the requirements of these highly regulated industries, but then if you are in one of these fields, you already know that.

Legal Considerations

The most easily accepted basic needs of a policy manual concern allowing the company to stay within the various legal requirements and considerations and still meet the objectives of the company.

For example, even if the idea of sex discrimination is the furthest thing from you mind, you should still make the declaration that it is not your company's policy to discriminate because of gender. If it is not your intention to discriminate, you have lost nothing; and if it is your intention to have suitability standards, you definitely should seek the advice of an attorney. As a practical matter, many states have covered these and other subjects, a reality providing an excellent reason to have a qualified legal specialist look over your company policies before submitting a policy manual to your employees for compliance. As this book is going to print, considerable speculation concerns what form AIDS legislation will ultimately fall into an illness or disability, one strongly protected from discrimination and the other less protected. Ultimately, the courts will make a determination of this issue. Until then, trust your own feelings on the preparation of your policy statement but also protect your rights by getting the best legal advice available. A more in-depth look at specific professional advice is covered under Specialized Help.

Basic Needs List

Topic	**Reason**
Employment Policy	Legal Requirement
Handicapped Policy	Legal Requirement
Holidays Policy	Legal Requirement
Jury Duty Policy	Legal Requirement
Military Leave Policy	Legal Requirement
Maternity/Paternity Leave Policy	Legal Requirement
Pay Period Policy	Legal Requirement
Religious Policy	Legal Requirement
Retirement Policy	Legal Requirement
Safety Policy	Legal Requirement
Sexual Harassment Policy	Legal Requirement
Workman's Compensation Policy	Legal Requirement

Although this is not the entire list from which to construct a policy manual it is a good area from which to start the process.

Goal Considerations

Defining the philosophy of the company and its attitude toward the customer provides benefits to the organization. Establishing that attitude correctly from the time an employee joins the organization often averts potential problems later. This would be the moment to state standards of excellence, establish codes of conduct, reiterate ethical values and proclaim social responsibility. This is the heart of your company, strong hearted companies flourish.

These bold statements indicate the care that you should use when setting the policy tone and content. Often those charged with the responsibility of establishing policy are competent but inexperienced, and they sometimes feel overwhelmed. But they should take heart. No doubt the framers of the Declaration of Independence had similar misgivings, and the Declaration of Independence has lasted 200 years.

Certain items rank high on any list used to formulate a policy manual. The following list is not meant as complete but only as a starting point.

Topic	**Consideration**
Attendance	Efficiency
Conduct	Morale
Customers	Efficiency
Discounts	Efficiency
Discipline	Morale
Reviews	Morale
Phone	Efficiency
Theft	Morale
Suggestions	Efficiency
Vacations	Morale
Working Hours	Efficiency

Any other considerations that you and your company decide are needed are just as important as those listed, perhaps more since you know what is important to your firm.

First Impressions

When developing your firm's policy manual, consider the image you wish your company to convey to your employees. Care given to what is said "between the lines" can avoid creating unnecessary and undesirable negative reactions from your employees. You may find the following guidelines helpful:

- When stating rules, be positive.
- When stating restrictions, give general reasons for them if possible.
- Helping your workers understand why rules are necessary makes compliance more palatable, and therefore, more likely.

A positive approach conveys the perception that you treat your employees as adults and that your policy manual is to help them understand your position on important matters of mutual interests, rather than a list of do's and do not's. Try thinking of your manual as a selling device through which you are promoting company policy and passing along sound recommendations. Then give your manual the same careful attention and the same professional appearance as the rest of your company's advertising programs.

Size of a Policy Manual

The size of a policy manual depends upon the scope of topics and depth of context. You will determine the size by the choices you make in various topics covered. It would be well to consider that the best interest of the company would be served by a less concise statement allowing for flexibility of operations and ease of understanding by employees.

I have seen manuals for major companies with as few as 20 half pages in booklet form and one that had over 1,000 pages in 10 loose-leaf binders. The smallest manual did not cover many areas that are structured by government regulations, and the largest manual did not allow much flexibility and in some cases seemed to have conflicting statements that could only confuse its employees. I could not even imagine the cost of allowing the firms employees to read and understand the contents of such a large document. The best answer probably lies somewhere between the two extremes, but most manuals that cover policy adequately are from 20 to 100 pages.

Policy Manual Format

The format of your policy manual offers an opportunity to demonstrate the professionalism of your organization. New employees usually receive a copy of the manual when hired, and an attractive, professional format can positively affect their perception of your firm while they are most open.

(a) Bound Book

For companies of more than 100 employees, the bound format is economical on a per employee basis and immediately projects the professionalism of an organization. The drawbacks of a bound presentation are the initial cost of production and the danger that certain information will become out dated, forcing the dumping of remaining manuals and higher individual cost.

(b) Loose-Leaf

The loose-leaf presentation is probably the most common. Its style ranges from a small folder to an elaborate binder and on a per cost basis is the highest. The first impression can be tailored to the immediate needs of the company. One of the advantages of this format is the ability to keep up-to-the-minute information available to all employees.

The loose-leaf form is my favorite if used with a routing sheet to all employees affected as changes happen. The main copy is usually located in a central office, and a master list of employees who have read and acknowledged the manual is kept to assure that all requirements are met.

For large corporations this procedure is not very practical because of the amount of detail work required, and the cost related to the tasks would be hard to justify.

Outside Assistance

You will cover many topics outside of your particular sphere of expertise. Because of the time and money required to learn everything related to each facet of specialization, the prudent individual usually avails himself or herself of someone who has already demonstrated abilities in the needed field. Obviously, a working knowledge of first aid is insufficient background to perform neurological surgery. To a lesser extent that analogy applies to what you will be doing if you attempt to complete the sensitive project of putting your company's policies into format without proper assistance. The amount and type of assistance is up to your own discretion and your allocated budget. The following categories include some of the sources that can direct you to good information. (You will probably want to start at the local library.)

Librarians

The single most important source of raw data is the library. The sheer amount of knowledge contained in a local library is such that most competent librarians hold a special degree in library sciences and have many years of hands-on and hand-holding experience to their credit.

State and Federal Agencies

Since any policy manual you finally decide upon has to pass muster with the people charged with seeing that you are complying with certain policies to begin with, why not ask for their assistance in reviewing your rough drafts and especially your final draft? Although some members of any bureaucracy are not driven by customer satisfaction, and do not worry about complaints causing a threat to their job security, many of these people are responsive and considerate. Find one who can and wants to help. It's to your advantage.

Academic Environments

Many of the finest minds are found in the teaching profession. (My dream of a think tank is my local college.) Even though professors have fixed schedules and a multitude of duties, they are almost always willing to offer advice; and if they cannot personally assist you, they may be able to offer the name of a gifted graduate assistant.

Legal

Although I am adamant that you should consult with a qualified legal expert, I suggest seeking a lawyer's advice as a final (rather than the first) step. I also suggest that you have a completely revised and fully completed text for the lawyer's use. Any detail work you accomplish will be well served by reducing the time to implement a policy and the amount of money a legal practioner charges.

Insurance Personnel

Your insurance company has a great interest in your company's policy. After all, if your employees make bad judgments, the insurance company pays. Insurance personnel will be able to make comments on a number of topics including workman's compensation, liability statements, company vehicles, drugs, alcohol, theft, and accidents. You are already paying for your insurance. You might be surprised at the amount of help the insurance company can provide.

Financial Advisors

Sometimes your financial matters are handled by people other than a CPA, but if you do employ a CPA then by all means seek his or her advice. If CPAs feel that the information they have is up to date and complete they will not have any problem responding; otherwise, don't expect any answers to hard questions. They make their living by not making mistakes, and you can generally rely on the information they offer.

Consultants

Only under limited circumstances would I feel comfortable recommending the use of a consultant. Those conditions are (1) you would lose money developing a policy yourself because of time spent outside your normal activities, (2) you do not have the ability to oversee closely enough the completion of a policy manual, or (3) the key working members of management feel that a consultant would produce the most objective policy. If you do ultimately decide to go this route, then review his or her recommendations very cautiously. Your mind is equally as good as that of a consultant and you know your company and all its peculiarities better than any consultant ever could.

CHAPTER 3

ADMINSTRATIVE ISSUES AND RELATED TOPICS WITH EXAMPLES

Attendance

Although it is not recommended that any employee have the right to come and go at will, some of the newer flexible work hours have shown surprising increases in efficiency by having employees at work when they are at their highest levels of productivity and are concerned with business, not who is going to pick up the children.

Any specific policy detailing the number of permitted absences or tardy appearances of employees is not advised. By limiting your policy statement to the need for regular attendance and punctuality, you retain the flexibility to exercise judgment on an individual basis.

Option #1

Punctual and consistent attendance is an important factor in determining an employee's continuation and advancement in the company. If an emergency requires an employee to leave the premises during working hours, the supervisor must first be notified. When an employee knows in advance that he or she must be absent from work, the supervisor should be notified before that time.

Employees should write down their supervisor's home phone number so that he or she may be called if necessary. Time lost by salaried employees as a result of repeated tardiness may be deducted from an employee's salary.

Option #2

The policy of this company concerning attendance is meant to encourage you to be as dependable as possible. Part of our image to our customers is the way you attend to their needs, and a great portion of that view of us is based on your being here on time and every work day. If you know in advance of future reasons for your absence from work, notify your supervisor so he can distribute his personnel resources. Remember that the company is committed to all our mutual needs. If an emergency arises, notify your supervisor immediately. Not only does this allow the company to make adjustments for your absence, but we are concerned about you and may be able to offer support to help meet your needs.

Option #3

All of us have occasions when it is necessary to be absent from our work. It is our policy to support employee needs in this regard. If you must absent yourself from work for any reason, notify your supervisor. Good employees are this company's best asset. We want your cooperation, and part of that is your reliable attendance. This company has a history of dependability because of the excellence of its employees and we need your support in this.

Repeated tardiness or absenteeism are viewed as unacceptable. Excessive tardiness can affect personal reviews and in some cases may be cause for disciplinary action or dismissal.

Option #4

If you know in advance of a need to miss work, notify your supervisor so that you will not be subject to a poor personal review. A necessary absence will cause him/her to wonder if you are dependable if you do not try to notify him. Proper notification allows him to take steps to maintain his responsibilities, and he/she will appreciate any assistance you can provide to help him/her meet those responsibilities.

If an emergency requires that you leave work, notify your supervisor. Supervisors are instructed to be supportive and to allow any employee to attend to an emergency. Explanations can be more easily understood after the emergency is over than during your crisis.

Company Meetings

Company meetings are expensive events due to both the loss of work that would otherwise be produced and to the actual cost of employees' wages for that time period. To complicate the issue, employees rarely comprehend the costs involved and so lack motivation to attend or observe punctuality. In addition, when other pressing matters have a higher priority, members of management may occasionally be absent from meetings if they already know the contents of the agenda or if the agenda's content does not affect them directly. (Management sometimes fails to recognize that the absence of notable managers may cause other employees to put less credence in the importance of meetings.) Therefore, writing a policy that is fair and equitable for everyone—members of management, other employees, and the company itself—can be a challenging task.

Because management legitimately must miss an occasional meeting, you may consider it in the company's best interest to be general on the topic of attendance in your written policy. You may then want to make managers aware that their presence at meetings sets a strong example and that when what is fair and equitable for one employee does not seem to apply to all, morale can suffer.

Option #1

Company meetings for certain employees will be held during normal working hours at times designated by management. The purpose of such meetings is for the dissemination of information, the solution of common problems, and the advancement of knowledge and understanding of the employees of the company. Attendance at such meetings is mandatory unless excused in advance by a supervisor.

Option #2

A monthly meeting will be scheduled for management personnel for the first Monday of each month. The purpose for meetings will include discussing departments, budgets, problems, responsibilities, and department suggestions. Each department shall have regularly scheduled meetings with supervisory personnel. Attendance at such meetings is mandatory unless excused in advance by a supervisor.

Option #3

Employee meetings and sales meetings will be conducted regularly by the manager to keep employees well-informed about products and company policy and to answer employees' questions. Attendance at such meetings is mandatory unless excused in advance by a supervisor.

Option #4

Staff meetings shall be had at regularly stated intervals. The time of such meetings and the person responsible for them shall be designated by management. The purpose of such meetings is for the dissemination of information, the solution of common problems, and the advancement of knowledge and understanding of the employees of the company. Persons designated to attend staff meetings will not absent themselves therefrom except when excused by management. Note: Meetings are held at all branches on Tuesday afternoons from 5:30 p.m. until 6:30 p.m. for all employees, except on the first Tuesday of each month, at which time meetings are held in designated meeting rooms for all employees from all branches. These evening meetings will begin at 7:30 p.m. and last until 9:30 p.m. Attendance at all Tuesday meetings is required for stipulated personnel. Absence without advance permission may be considered grounds for immediate dismissal.

Conduct

Of all the topics listed in this manual, employee conduct is one of the most abused and least understood by managers. When preparing a policy concerning conduct, it might be valuable if you use the approach that this subject, about the way one acts, if abused could lead to termination. A stronger statement could include a separate list of needs and address it from a point of equitable fairness.

It is also wise to note that what an employee does on his/her own time may not be censured or regulated by the company unless it impacts directly upon the company in some manner.

Option #1

All of us prefer to work in a job situation where our fellow employees cooperate and respect one another's rights. The company is convinced that good judgement and common courtesy are a necessary part of every employee's work habits.

Option #2

All of us can accomplish our work effectively only with the cooperation and respect of our fellow employees. Every employee is expected to exercise good judgement and show cooperation and courtesy in dealing with his fellow employees and with the public. In addition to these general principles, the Company has found it necessary to establish certain specific prohibitions. Without excluding other grounds, any of the following may be considered grounds for disciplinary action or discharge:

1. Neglect or disregard of assigned duties.
2. Leaving the job without permission during regular working hours.
3. Habitual absence or tardiness.
4. Falsification of information on a timecard or punching another employee's timecard.
5. Abuse of lunch hour privileges.
6. Loitering on the job.
7. Drinking of alcoholic beverages on the job.
8. Immoral, obscene, or indecent conduct or language.
9. Gambling on company premises.
10. Fighting.
11. Soliciting, collecting funds, or loaning money without approval.
12. Participating in unauthorized meetings or gatherings on company time and company property.
13. Abuse of company property (e.g., loss of tools, careless use of machinery or trucks, or disposing of reuseable items).
14. Repeated garnishments.
15. Unauthorized use of company vehicles or equipment.
16. Theft of company property or property of fellow employees, or other dishonesty.
17. Taking company property, records, or confidential information from the premises without permission.
18. Possession of firearms or explosives on company property, unless specifically authorized.
19. Violating safety rules: (e.g., failure to wear safety equipment and failure to report injuries).
20. On-the-job use of marijuana or hard drugs, or off duty use of such drugs in a way that affects job performance.

Option #3

- Use of profanity of any sort, on or off the sales floor, is prohibited.
- No eating or drinking will be allowed while in sales area.
- Salesmen will avoid placing hands in pockets while waiting on customers.
- Personal phone calls during working hours should be avoided.
- Salesmen should avoid any unnecessary talking in groups, calling loudly, or joking on the job in the sales area.
- All employees will conduct themselves in a businesslike manner at all times.
- Employees are required to maintain good personal grooming habits at all times. Hair must be cut regularly and kept neat. Men must be cleanly shaven daily. Goatees, beards, and excessive sideburns are prohibited. Mustaches must be kept trimmed and neat.
- Smoking of cigarettes is permissible on duty. We ask that those of you who do smoke follow these rules:
  1. If a customer is smoking, then feel free to light up.
  2. If he is not smoking and you wish to do so, then ask the customer in a pleasant manner, "Do you mind if I smoke?" This is only common courtesy. Be careful while smoking not to blow smoke in the customer's face. Do not allow cigarettes to hang out of the corner of your mouth while talking with the customer. Cigars and cigarillos are not allowed while on duty.

Option #4

The following conduct can be considered cause for disciplinary action:

1. Loitering or loafing—Deliberate loitering or loafing during working hours will not be tolerated.

2. Inattention to assigned duties.
3. Refusal to work on job assigned.
4. Walking off the job without permission during regular working hours.
5. Drinking between 8 a.m. and 5 p.m. on working days.
6. Abuse of lunch hour privileges.
7. Dishonesty, stealing company products, materials, or stealing from fellow employees.
8. Fighting during working hours.
9. Disregard for company materials (i.e., loss of tools, careless use of machinery or trucks, disposing of reuseable items).
10. Excessive garnishments levied.
11. Unauthorized use of company vehicles or equipment.

Option #5

We know that all decent people prefer to work where folks respect each other and work together in peace and harmony.

We are sure that each of you knows the difference between right and wrong. Therefore, regulations covering the common decencies will not become work rules here.

However, there are some work rules we wish to mark clear. Employees will be subject to disciplinary action for any of the following offenses:

1. Engaging in horseplay, running, scuffling, or throwing things.
2. Failure to observe parking and traffic regulations on company property.
3. Being tardy or absent without authorization.
4. Contributing to unsanitary conditions or poor housekeeping.

5. Operating, using, or possessing machines, tools, or equipment to which the employee has not been assigned or while not performing assigned work.
6. Causing damage of material or equipment due to carelessness.
7. Wasting time loitering or leaving place of work during working hours without permission.
8. Gambling on company premises.
9. Violating a safety rule or safety practice.
10. Carelessness affecting personal safety.
11. Threatening, intimidating, coercing, or interfering with fellow employees.
12. Making false, vicious, or malicious statements about any employee, the company, or its products.
13. Leaving the plant during working hours without permission.
14. Failure to follow company job instructions, verbal or written.
15. Misusing, destroying, or damaging any company property or property of any employees.
16. Deliberately restricting output.
17. Provoking or instigating a fight or fighting during working hours or on company property.
18. Reporting for work under the influence of alcohol or drugs.
19. Insubordination.
20. Falsifying company records.
21. Knowingly punching another employee's timecard; having one's time card punched by another; altering timecard for any reason.
22. Possessing firearms or explosives on company premises without authorization.

23. Smoking except in specified areas at specified times.
24. Theft of any company, government, or employee's property.
25. Removal of articles of company property without written authorization.
26. Drinking any alcoholic beverages on the premises or on company time.
27. Immoral conduct or indecency.
28. Taking merchandise off the shelf for use on company grounds without approval from supervisor.
29. Purchasing of merchandise at a discount without going through your supervisor.

Option #6

Since the impression you make will be the customer's impression of the entire company, we emphasize good business conduct at all times. Employees should avoid talking in groups, visiting with friends, or calling loudly. Idle talk or joking on the job and smoking in sales areas are not considered consistent with the company's policies of courtesy and good business conduct.

Option #7

You are directed to control your temper during the work day. Never use obscene or vulgar language in a customer's presence. If overheard, and the client is offended, you will be discharged. Excessive horseplay or loudness on the property of a client will not be tolerated. If you are greeted by a client, please answer clearly, politely, and SMILE. If questioned by a client on some matter of which you have no knowledge, refer the client to your foreman or the office—POLITELY.

Never offer information about work unless certain of what you speak.

Option #8

As a representative of the company, all employees are expected to be neat in appearance. Each department manager will set standards according to clientele dealt with.

Foolhardy acts, joking around, or horseplay will not be tolerated. Drinking of alcoholic beverages, as well as use of narcotics is prohibited. Any such acts of misconduct will be grounds for immediate dismissal.

Option #9

PERSONAL LIFE—The company expects all employees to live in such a manner that their personal life neither affects their work harmfully nor reflects on the company's reputation in a detrimental manner. But your personal life is your own to lead as you wish, and the company will not interfere with it in any way.

The company believes that it and all its employees should obey all laws and live in such a manner that both will be assets to their community.

Confidential Information

Since the advent of the "Information Age," many companies have recognized their own information as a company asset to be kept safe. Even a small dirt hauling company could suffer severe damage should information concerning their bids become known to competitors. Although your firm may not be in a field where information is thought of as having value, consider the recent reported experience of a Washington law firm.

Suspecting a leak of confidential information, the law firm hired a private investigator. The revelations of that investigation led to the entire reorganization of how information was handled and who would be allowed into certain areas of their offices.

A portion of the investigator's report told of a temporary-help secretary with computer word processing skills who was selling up-to-date financial data, in micro disk format, concerning an investor client to another firm; an overly helpful janitor "who didn't mind helping" the "overworked secretaries" make copies of important documents and who was making extra copies and carrying them out at night with the trash for sale to various companies, including; a newspaper, and building maintenance workers who were removing unused and stored office equipment for sale to private individuals in the classified section of a newspaper. The final blow was that a coffee service vendor had removed over $2,000 from petty cash without being caught because the partners commonly removed small sums for personal use and did not want to cry "wolf" if it might expose their own personal irregularities.

Admittedly, the above example is an extreme case of poor management, but think about the of damage that can be caused by the loss of confidential information, especially with the growing use of small computers. (This entire book is contained on two disks three and one-half inches wide.) It is important to consider the stance your firm should take about handling information.

Option #1

It is the policy of this company that any and all information about our business be treated as strictly confidential and further, since our clients expect confidential conduct, that any work done for them be treated with the same understanding and agreement.

Option #2

Any information concerning customers, suppliers, taxes, bookkeeping, or other financial data is confidential and shall not be released in any way to anyone who is not an employee of this firm, unless authorized by your supervisor.

Option #3

The categories of information considered to be the property of this company does not allow for their individual listing. This company does not allow any employee to give out any information about our firm, its clients or employees without the written consent of a member of management.

Option #4

It is a policy of this firm and a condition of employment that all employees treat any information about this firm, its customers, and our financial data as proprietary. Good judgment is to be exercised at all times. If you wish more detailed directions or if your position entails more than passing access to the inner workings of confidential information, you will be asked to execute an agreement of confidential conduct. If you do not feel comfortable with this requirement, consult your supervisor immediately.

Example of Possible Contract Clause

As a portion of my agreement to work for the company, I agree not to reveal to any person, unless authorized by the company or its duly authorized officials, any confidential information concerning its or their intentions, processes, methods, or any of its confidential affairs; and I further agree that during my employment I will not engage in any activities competitive with the activities of the company, and I will not assist others in any such activities.

Copyright and Patent Policy

In the late 1970s, I worked for a engineering firm primarily involved in interior industrial pollution control. One of my co-workers, got an idea to connect a common household vacuum to our pollution control equipment, simple but very workable. The company did not profit from the idea, due to their own oversight and poor policy. Many other products such as the Crescent wrench (which was thought of by an employee of a retail chain) or Liquid Paper (which was thought of by a secretary) could have benefitted the original companies that these people worked for, yet did that did not happen because of poor policy.

Some company advisers have erroneously believed that even if this topic is not publicly addressed, that courts will find in favor of the company. However, an attorney will probably tell you that it is in the best interest of all concerned to be aware of what is normally expected of companies and employees so that misunderstandings do not occur.

A policy concerning the development or conception of new ideas or products could become a valuable asset. Although you may not immediately foresee a need for this, consider that all of your employees have the ability to conceive of ways that may improve the efficiency of products they work with.

Option #1

The conception of new products or ideas directly related to our industry and which are developed with knowledge or resources supplied by this company are considered to be the property of this company. We have developed an awards program to foster the concept of innovation among our employees. If you think of a way to improve our efficiency or the efficiency of our industry or perceive the possibility of new product, it is our commitment to support that development.

Option #2

We are always looking to our employees to be leaders in this industry; that is one of the reasons you were chosen to work here. The conceiving of new ideas is part of the lifeblood of our company. Ideas and products fostered with knowledge or resources are the property of this company.

Option #3

We have shown our belief and trust in your creativity and abilities through your employment, and we need your commitment to foster the growth of the company. One area not often thought of as a center of growth is the bringing to life of new ways of doing things. You are encouraged to constantly be aware of possibilities for improving productivity. It is this company's policy that the development of new products or ideas by our employees is the property of this company. The development and growth that all our employees receive from new concepts will be shown at personnel wage/salary review time.

Option #4

Patents or intellectual property developed by an employee with knowledge or other resources derived while employed by this company are the property of this company.

Possible Contract Agreement

In consideration of the compensation paid to me by the company and of the position which I occupy and which brings me into contact with the activities of the company in connection with its engineering, research, and development work and its manufacturing operations, I hereby agree that any inventions or improvements that I may conceive, make, invent, or suggest, solely or jointly with others, during the period covering my employment by the company, and relating to any matter or thing pertaining to the business or activities of the company, including said engineering, research, and development work and said manufacturing operations, shall become the absolute property of said company, and I will at the request of said company execute any and all papers and documents pertaining to such inventions and improvements that said company may consider necessary or helpful in the prosecution of applications for patent thereon, or in perfecting title to such inventions and the patent right thereon in said company; and should I leave the employment of the company, I will at any time thereafter and upon request, execute all such lawful papers as it may desire, all expense incident to the preparation and use of such papers to be borne by said company. I further agree to disclose promptly to the company all such inventions and improvements.

Example

We have developed an awards program to foster the concept of innovation among our employees, If you think of a way to improve our efficiency or the efficiency of our industry or perceive the possibility of new product, it is our commitment to support that development.

Company Credit Cards

Company credit cards are one of those controversial issues that have many risk management people having nightmares about. If your company has company credit cards, even a card from a gasoline company, then you need to address this topic. If you set guidelines for control early you will save effort, litigation and money latter.

I have been asked by a clerk in a 'mini-market' type gas station if I wanted to place merchandise on my company credit card! It made me wonder how often this happens, so I started examining old receipts and found that over half of them had only the bottom portion with total filled in.

One company cancelled all company credit cards after an ex-employee charged $8,000 in vacation expenses and quit upon return to his home. Litigation is still pending, and the company regrets that they did not have any written guidelines.

Option #1

Company credit cards are issued to certain authorized employees to use for official company business only. Misuse can lead to dismissal.

Option #2

We strive to help our employees to be as efficient as possible. With that in mind we have issued company credit cards to authorized employees. The issue of these cards is a sign of our trust in you and a measure of your dependability. Receipts will be turned into your supervisor immediately upon return to work. Company credit cards are authorized for company expenses only, and any unauthorized use will call for immediate dismal and possible criminal prosecution.

Option #3

Company credit cards are issued for the use of authorized personnel in the development of company goals. Unauthorized use will be grounds for dismissal. Receipts will be turned in with normal expense reports. Receipts not turned in cannot be approved and therefore will not paid by the company.

Option #4

Our company credit cards are to be treated with the same safeguards as you would treat confidential company documents or expensive company assets. They are entrusted to your care, and you are responsible for their security and use.

All receipts are to be turned in with your normal expense reports. They are to be used for company business only. Improper or unauthorized use will not be acceptable, and employees will be subject to dismissal if found negligent in this regard.

Employee Discipline

The matter of employee discipline is of concern to all employees. It is one of their methods of judging equitable and fair treatment by the company. When making your company's policy on discipline, make certain that all employees understand the need to have disciplinary measures and that they recognize the fairness of the policy.

Check with state and local authorities to make certain that the policy you decide upon is in compliance with current labor laws.

Option #1

All employees are subject to the company's discipline policy. Your supervisor will counsel you, and a member of management will be present at any discipline discussion. We have established the various work rules not to make your job harder but to help insure the safety and efficiency of you and those around you. Only by your help and observance of these rules can we meet our insurance requirements, stay within the various safety and health standards, and comply with labor laws.

Option #2

Many federal, state, and local laws require our compliance, so many, in fact, that it is not practicable for the company to expect our employees to be aware of them all, especially since laws have a tendency to change fairly often. Thus, it is our responsibility to stay within these rules for your benefit. We, therefore, expect you to comply with all posted notices. If you wish to know more about any rule or why it is in effect here, ask your supervisor, and he will be glad to explain it to you. Any employee who does not follow these rules will be disciplined by a member of management.

Option #3

Not all companies have the same high standards we do. Our company is dedicated to the safety and high standards of our employees, and we require all employees to adhere strictly to the posted rule and regulations of this company. If you want to understand why a rule is in effect, ask your supervisor to explain. Our policy is that any employee who violates the posted rules will be disciplined as the severity of the violation dictates.

Option #4

This company's policy on discipline requires all employees to observe the posted company rules as a part of their employment. Any employee who does not comply with those rules will be disciplined as the severity of the offense dictates.

Information Disclosure

The disclosure of small amounts of information by a company about employment history or about customers has caused many companies to pay dearly. Lawsuits have been brought and won on a variety of seemingly insignificant statements. Companies would do well to consider what potential gain may be had by discussing any subject about its employees or customers, against the possibility of risk of lawsuit should you unknowingly make a false statement—or a statement that you know is true but cannot prove to the satisfaction of a court.

If you adopt a policy of total or limited confidentiality, not allowing any aspect of ex-employee history, current employee history, or customer history to be revealed or allowing only the fact that they have had an association with your organization, then you will limit the amount of risk to your firm. In some cases those concerned may wish you to disclose information about their activities with your organization, but you are under no obligation to do so.

Should you find a reason to release information to someone outside your firm, it should be essential for you to obtain a written agreement from the party concerned that gives you permission and holds you blameless from any harm such disclosure may cause.

If you decide to release information about employees, past employees, or customers, be careful what you decide to release. Items concerning sexual preference, religion or age should be avoided.

Option #1

We do not allow any disclosure of any information, of any nature, concerning employees, past employees, or customers.

Option #2

The only information allowed for release about employees, past employees, or customers is that they have had a relationship with this organization.

Option #3

Only when a signed "Release of Information" form is on file will we release any information about employees, past employees, or customers.

Leave of Absence

A leave of absence can be for any number of things but is normally intended for hardship. Some instances may require a time limit be placed upon the leave to allow the company to protect itself. Occasionally it might be beneficial to consider a leave in lieu of allowing an extremely good employee quit for educational reasons.

Option #1

An unpaid leave of absence for cause may be granted by the company providing it does not seriously disrupt operations. A request for leave will be presented to the Supervisor and Personnel Department. Such leave will be discussed and determined on an individual basis.

Option #2

There will be instances when it will be in the best interest of both the company and an employee for the company to authorize a leave of absence. Because of our present vacation, holidays, group insurance, and retirement programs, based on continuous service, leaves of absence should not exceed 90 days. Your department head must request authorization from the Personnel Department for any such leave of absence.

Group insurance benefits may be continued while on leave if advance arrangements are made for payment of premiums.

If you are a member of the retirement plan, all benefits will be held to your credit during the leave.

A record will be made in the Personnel Department of your expected date of return from leave. If you do not return on or before the specified date of return, all vacation privileges, retirement plan benefits, and group insurance protection must be cancelled.

Option #3

Leaves of absence may be arranged during off season for sufficient reason. If you have a problem and wish a leave, see your supervisor, and he will consider arranging it for you.

Option #4

A leave of absence for cause may be granted by the company provided it does not seriously disrupt operations. A request for leave of absence will be presented to the Supervisor in writing. An illness or accident not connected with employment, which requires staying away from work more than five consecutive days, will require a leave of absence. A leave of absence will also be granted for death in the immediate family (wife, husband, parents, or children) of not to exceed five days without pay. An employee who fails to report for work the first workday after the expiration of this leave will be considered to have quit. Holiday pay will not be paid for a holiday which occurs during a leave of absence. An employee returning from a leave of absence will be returned to his former job if practical.

Option #5

Leaves of absence may be granted for reasonable lengths of time, without pay, based on management's judgment as to the necessity of the leave and always on an individual basis. Although the company has set no absolute maximum, 60 days is usually considered the maximum period of time for a leave of absence.

Leaves of absence normally will not be considered until an employee has had at least six months' continuous full-time employment. A maximum of two weeks' leave of absence may granted after six months, but less than one year, of employment.

Requests for leaves of absence must be submitted to supervisors in writing.

Option #6

A leave of absence for cause may be granted by the company provided it does not seriously disrupt operations. An illness or accident not connected with employment, which requires staying away from work more than five consecutive days, will require a leave of absence. A leave of absence will also be granted for death in the immediate family (wife, husband, parents, children) not to exceed five days without pay. An employee who fails to report for work the first workday following this leave will be considered to have quit. Holiday pay will not be paid for a holiday which occurs during a leave of absence.

License Requirements

In industries and professions that mandate the licensing or certification of employees (such as lawyers, engineers, pesticide applicators, electricians or doctors), the management should address this requirement in a policy statement. Your intent is to make certain that only qualified individuals are authorized to perform certain functions.

Proper licensing and certification reduce the liability of your company to some degree, and you will be placing a portion of responsibility on the employee to keep his credentials in order. Do not be deluded into a false sense of security: your company is responsible for the actions and suitability of its employees at all times. This includes certifications and licenses required to perform work.

Option #1

It is the policy of this organization that employees in positions requiring certification or licensing are responsible for notifying their supervisor in the event of loss or expiration of that certification or license.

Option #2

This company is constantly trying to make certain that its employees are the best in our field. Should you have any change in the licenses or certifications required in the performance of your position, you are to make this information known to your supervisor immediately.

Option #3

Many of the types of work performed by us require licenses or certifications, and it is the responsibility of the employee to keep his supervisor appraised of the status of his individual qualifications to perform certain work. If you are directed to perform work that you do not hold credentials for, immediately notify your supervisor and do not attempt to perform such work.

Option #4

Our continuing education programs are intended to allow our personnel to maintain the highest standards in the industry. It is the responsibility of the employee to keep his supervisor informed in any change regarding his licensing of certifications to perform certain types of work. Employees are not permitted to perform work without the correct credentials in force for the type of work directed.

Moonlighting

Full-time employees making decent wages may seek moonlighting for any number of reasons, but the most common is the working toward a specific goal such as a house or the retirement of an unexpected debt.

Some companies adopt the attitude that a full-time employee can have no interest other than their own company, while other companies endeavor to understand the reason for a second job. Companies that have sought to understand the employee's point of view, have achieved some remarkable results.

In one case, a company offered an employee supplementary wages for performing duties outside of his regular responsibilities. Consequently, that employee, feeling that his company cared for him and his family and that he mattered, became a much more loyal employee.

In another case, an employee was terminated for part-time employment even though he had sought and obtained his supervisor's approval. This ex-employee has very few nice things to say about that firm: they made a poor decision and earned the animosity of that employee for life.

Option #1

Moonlighting is the practice of working a second job for another employer in addition to working for the company. You may not engage in the sales of goods or services offered by this company in any of its division as a representative of another firm or yourself. However, it is not consistent with the company's need to have you represent the company all of the time, both on and off the job. Moonlighting may be permitted if there is no conflict of interest and if it does not affect your work performance here. See your supervisor for approval.

Option #2

The Company will not permit you to engage after hours, on Saturday, Sunday, or others holidays, in any work that is also done by the company. If you fail to comply, you will be discharged. It is the responsibility of every employee to promote work for the company to help insure his own job.

Option #3

Check with your supervisor for approval before accepting a second job. We understand that each case is different and will make decisions on a case-by-case basis.

Option #4

If you feel that you want or need extra work, check with your supervisor. Although labor laws may prevent the company arranging for extra work, we may be able to offer assistance in other ways. At least let us try.

News Bulletin

A policy about a newsletter is not considered a high priority by most managers. However, a news bulletin can serve as the single most vital link to communication between management and line employees. Some meaning is naturally lost when all communication from top management to line employees passes through the chain of command. Perhaps a manager assumes that employees are already aware of the communication, or he may decide that a particular aspect of the communication does not affect the line employees and consequently fails to convey information to them.

For this reason many companies publish a periodic newsletter. All communications are made available to all employees in the format that management wants it conveyed. A particular side benefit is that this document could become an important vehicle for explaining known policies, attitudes, and directions should a legal need arise.

Option #1

Employees will receive the company news bulletin from time to time. This bulletin is the company's way of helping all of us know one another better. Through this newsletter, the company hopes it can become a part of each employee's family in much the same way all employees are welcomed as part of the company family.

Noncompetition Agreements

Because of the confidential nature of some positions and the specialized information handled in these positions, some companies have found that unfair advantage can be gained by competitors who raid their work force. Due to these concerns noncompetition agreements have emerged to help alleviate this problem. Care should be taken when considering which positions are to be covered and how they are to be addressed.

It is possible to restrict activities of ex-employees in various ways, but the most common are geographic, chronological, and specified activities or a combination of these. Geographic restrictions normally define the area where the individual may not engage in work that would harm the company. In the quickly changing business environment, current knowledge is vital and a chronological restriction will limit your firm's risk concerning information subject to change. Specific activity restrictions apply more to secret or confidential processes such as manufacturing or research.

No options are listed because you should obtain specialized legal advice for guidelines.

Personnel Records

Employee records are needed for reasons varying from tax information to maintaining compliance with insurance requirements. But certain types of information are being deemed an invasion of privacy. In maintaining records, avoid crossing over into the personal privacy area. If you are unsure why various bits of information are needed, ask a competent authority. Also explain to your employees why you are requesting information and request voluntary compliance.

Option #1

The company maintains a personnel file on all employees. If any employee has a change of address, telephone number, marital or family status, change of insurance beneficiary, or person to be notified in case of emergency, report the change to the office as soon as possible. This file is also used to record lateness, absence, records of work, and information necessary to fulfill requirements for merit raises in pay. It is to your best interest to notify the office of any and all changes.

Option #2

It is very important that all changes of name, address, telephone number, or dependents to be reported without delay. This is necessary so that you or your family can be reached quickly in cases of sickness, accident, or emergency work. Your payroll, insurance, and personnel records should be kept up-to-date by contacting your supervisor.

Option #3

In order that employment records may be kept up-to-date, employees are requested to notify the company immediately in any of the following cases:

1. When the employee changes address or telephone number
2. When any change occurs in dependency status

Option #4

Employees should report promptly any change of address, telephone number, or family status to their supervisor, who will adjust the records and forward the information to the Payroll Department. This is important both for company records and in cases of personal emergency.

Personnel Reviews

Timely wage and salary reviews and promotions may be the area most often overlooked by management, although it is probably one of the most cussed and discussed topics of employee concern. When this matter is ignored, an employee may respond with apathetic work habits and undesirable malcontent, attitudes that can spread to other employees and affect the morale of an entire work force. Even in lean periods, it is a good policy to evaluate employees even when unable to increase wages. Honest appreciation of good work almost always receives a positive response.

Option #1

There is opportunity to advance with the company. It is the policy to fill vacancies by upgrading or promoting from within, whenever present employees are qualified. Factors considered in connection with promotions include:

- Performance
- Attendance
- Attitude
- Leadership
- Job Qualifications and Training
- Length of Employment

Option #2

All hourly employees will be evaluated twice each year during the months of January and July. The company policy is that the evaluation should be an open exchange in which both parties freely participate and during which the supervisor points out the employee's strong points as well as areas for improvement. The results of this process are committed to a rating form which becomes a part of the employee's personnel folder.

Option #3

Good work, attitude, and attendance pay off. At regular intervals the company looks at the job employees are doing and rates them. Supervisors rate the quality and quantity of work. They also rate job knowledge, adaptability, dependability, attitude, and safety and housekeeping practices. These factors determine an employee's advancement.

Option #4

Present employees will be considered for promotion before new employees are hired for the vacancy. Employees with the required knowledge, skill, ability, interest, and physical fitness will be given a trial test when practical. Length of service will be a factor in determining promotions. Available vacancies will be a factor in determining promotions. Any vacancy likely to last more than 30 days which is not due to temporary causes and which the company decides should be filled, will be filled by promotion of present employees, if reasonably qualified. The company will select the employees to be transferred or promoted to a vacancy from among those who have requested transfer to the vacancy and who have demonstrated their ability to do the job. The company will hire a new employee to fill a vacancy to which no qualified employee has requested consideration for.

Option #5

Promotions are based on merit. When an opening occurs, the person who has the best all-around record gets the job. Among the things we consider are performance on present and previous jobs, ability to take on added responsibility, attendance record, time with the company, and experience and training in the field when the opening occurs.

One important thing that we have noticed about promotions is that very often the difference between the person who gets the promotion and the one that doesn't is very small. Many times the person who gets promoted is one who showed a little more interest in his work and was a little more accurate on his job, was absent a day or two less, or worked a little faster. These little daily differences often make the big difference when it comes to promotions.

It is the company policy to promote from within whenever possible. This is good for you because it means more opportunity for a better job and higher pay. It is good for us because if you have these opportunities, you will be better satisfied. This generally means that you will do a better job.

We hire from outside only when we need special experience and skills not available within our own organization.

Your future can be as bright as you wish to make it. The future of any individual is determined by his desire to succeed, his ambition, and his willingness to work a little harder than the other fellow.

Option #6

Promotion within the company shall be made on the basis of experience, education, and service. As openings arise, qualified personnel within the company shall be given adequate opportunity for advancement prior to hiring new personnel.

A company employee may be hired for or promoted to the job classifications shown in the following list. Your classification in advancement will be determined by your manager as recommended by the supervisor or foreman over you:

Classifications:

Supervisor (Ia)
Supervisor (Ib)
Foreman (IIa)
Foreman (IIb)
Foreman (IIc)
Crew Chief (IIIa)
Crew Chief (IIIb)
(other)

New employees initially hired qualifying for one of the employment classifications shall receive the rate for that class. After six months he may be advanced according to his ability to perform.

All full-time employees will have their work evaluated twice each year by management. Such evaluation will answer the employees' questions as to: (1) What are my job duties and responsibilities? (2) How am I doing? (3) What are my job goals for the future?

Pilfering

Pilfering, shoplifting, or theft of any kind is not condoned by any company, but you should consider the ramifications of instructing an employee to detain or arrest a person suspected of theft. It is more acceptable for trained police officers to handle this type of situation than it is to have your own personnel attempt to place themselves at risk. If violence happens to your employee or an innocent bystander, you may have opened your company to a lawsuit. The employee may state he was not trained to perform the function of security, and the customer may say that he was endangered unnecessarily. Your insurance company may have a few comments to the same effect.

Option #1

We do not feel our employees should take any direct action against thievery. If you see what appears to be a theft, you are to notify a supervisor, who will call police.

Option #2

Avoid falsely accusing a shopper of stealing. You must see the suspected shoplifter conceal the item either on his person or in his car. Moreover, you must watch him continuously if he is suspected of stealing, in order to make sure he has not discarded the item. You must make sure that he has not paid for the item. He may have paid for other items, and the only way you can prove that he has concealed something is to observe his conversation with a clerk or cashier. The shoplifter does not have to prove he is telling the truth; you have to prove he is lying.

Continuous observation of a suspicious person is important. Usually an experienced shoplifter is swift and sure in his movements. In such a case, one might say, "I have observed you continuously and you have ___ that you have not paid for." Generally the approach should be quiet and tactful, such as "Did you forget to pay for anything?" If the person will not give up the merchandise and drives away, you should note a description of the car and license number, then call the police immediately.

Two witnesses are better than one in apprehending shoplifters. Shoplifters, in general, are less apt to cause trouble if there are two witnesses instead of one.

If you should apprehend a shoplifter, it is best to use a quiet place off to one side of the sales floor and away from public view. If the shoplifter is a woman, always have another female present. Ask the shoplifter to place all stolen items on a desk or table. If he refuses, call the police, then watch him carefully for an attempt at discarding anything.

Always remember that false arrest can cost large sums—be sure you avoid this by taking the above steps when apprehending anyone for stealing.

Option #3

Certain losses are expected and taken into consideration when we develop our market prices. Our employees are the most important asset of this company and we do not wish to jeopardize their safety. Therefore, confronting a thief is not a policy we endorse nor condone. If you see what appears to be a theft, call the police.

Option #4

In the event that you see what appears to be a theft of our property, make mental notes of the occurrence, do not take any action against the suspected thief yourself. Call the police and your supervisor, then write down everything you possibly can concerning the theft.

Substance Abuse

The liability exposure, to a company, from an employee whose judgement is impaired due to the effects of drugs or alcohol can become expensive. A driver involved in an accident or an employee who incorrectly labels a hazardous product, can cause an impact on profitability and public relations. Some firms have recognized that a definite need exist to limit this risk. Even the most common of tasks carries with it certain responsibilities, and an impaired employee may not have the ability to ascertain the ramifications of his or her actions.

Your firm may have specialized needs. If you are unsure, as to what alternatives are available to your company, check with local, recognized groups that focus on specific problems. These groups have up-to-date information and are willing to help.

Option #1

This company is an affirmative action company and our employees are the heart of our company. We want to go the extra step to help any employee who is having a problem with drugs, alcohol, or mental stress. Contact your supervisor for details.

Option #2

The safety of our employees demands, the company take all measures possible to insure a safe work environment. Substance abuse could lead to possible hazards we can not tolerate. Substance abuse is a serious problem and we treat it as such. Any employee, who is determined to be a substance abuser, will be subject to immediate disciplinary action.

Option #3

The problems associated with substance abuse, make it necessary to mandate a policy of dismissal for any employee who is determined to be a substance abuser.

Option #4

Employees who have problems with drugs or alcohol are encouraged to seek the assistance of our personnel department, for enrollment in an affirmative action program. A determination will be made as to what restrictions need be applied for the safety of the employee and the company. Upon completion of the program the employee will be reinstated for normal responsibilities.

Supervisor/Foreman

A company's concept of the supervisors role can strengthen the company's ability to maintain high efficiency. The supervisor, at whatever level, deserves the company's strongest support and backing. You should make an active effort to prevent circumvention of this line of command so that employees under the supervisor's direction receive uniform instructions and clearly understand whose directions to follow.

A strong policy statement (provided for all employees when hired) demonstrates the degree of responsibility you place in your supervisors and clearly establishes a line of command and communication. In turn, supervisors will know that you trust their judgment and expect high standards.

Option #1

The supervisor is the person with whom employees will be in daily contact. He will evaluate employees periodically in terms of attendance, attitude, performance, and ability. His recommendations will be one of the most important factors in any merit pay increases. Should an employee have any questions or problems about company policy, or any other matter, he should talk with his supervisor. The supervisor reflects the thoughts of company management and has responsibility for making sure that operations are handled efficiently.

Option #2

Your immediate supervisor is the person you report to for job direction and responsibilities. Any changes about your functions or performance should be communicated to him at once. All decisions to direct you to another department or person are made by him. If there is a conflict or problem that you or he feels must be addressed by management, your supervisor is required to bring the matter to the attention of his superior at once, and those concerned will resolve it.

Option #3

Our supervisors are one of the greatest assets of this company. We have given them the responsibility of making sure that operations are done in as efficient a manner as possible, while requiring them to see that the highest standards of our industry are maintained. Employees are directed to report to their assigned supervisor for work assignments, schedules, and other changes affecting them.

Termination of Employment/Recall

It is important to check state and local law for specific time limits and procedures for termination of employment and payment of final wages. Although a company has the right to choose who may work for it, some states have regulations that, unless followed exactly, entitle an ex-employee state benefits and workman's compensation benefits that otherwise would not be granted.

A case example involves an employee who was terminated for dishonesty and theft. The ex-employee filed for workman's compensation benefits and unemployment benefits stating that he had been injured and could not work and that he had been fired without cause. Because a written employer response was not made in 14 days of his claim, all appeals by the employer were lost! (I am still mad at myself over that.)

Option #1

If an employee has been on the payroll for one year, but less than two years, one week's advance notice of termination will be given. The company may, at its discretion, apply one week's wage in lieu of notice. If an employee has been on the payroll two years or more, the company will give either two weeks' notice or pay two weeks' wage in lieu of notice. No notice need be given to probationary employees. No advance notice of termination or termination pay need be given if an employee is dismissed because of misconduct, insubordination, or failure to follow company rules.

Regular work will be provided as far as practicable. However, because of the seasonal nature of our business, at times layoffs are necessary. If a layoff should become necessary, employees will be laid off on the basis of their ability, attendance, length of service, and production records.

All departments will try to schedule work so that employees who must be laid off can be given adequate advance notice. However, it is recognized that there are times when economic conditions make it impossible to give such advance notice. Every effort will be made to call laid-off employees back to work as soon as possible. An employee who declines recall to his regular job will be considered to have quit.

Option #2

Steady and continued employment benefits both the employees and the company. However, we realize there are circumstances where it becomes necessary for an employee to terminate employment. The following are various types of terminations:

1. *Voluntary Resignation*

   An hourly paid employee is requested to give his supervisor at least five days' notice prior to actual termination. A salaried employee is requested to give at least 15 days (or more) notice.

2. *Layoff*

   Layoff may result from lack of work in a department. Prior to the layoff of any employee, every effort will be made to provide an opportunity for transfer to another department where the employee's skill and ability can be utilized. Employees being laid off will be given at least one week's notice or equivalent pay in lieu of notice. The company will also make every effort to rehire a laid-off employee when work in which his skills can be utilized becomes available.

3. *Discharges*

The company retains the right to discharge any employee. A discharged employee will receive his paycheck as soon as possible after termination in accordance with appropriate state laws. The company will give at least one week's notice of discharge, or equivalent pay in lieu of notice, except that no notice need be given to probationary employees, or to any employee dismissed because of misconduct, insubordination, or failure to follow company rules.

Option #3

If you have been on the payroll one year, but less than two years, you will be given one week's advance notice of termination. The company may, at its discretion, pay one week's wage in lieu of notice.

If you have been on the payroll two years or more, the company will give you either two weeks' notice or pay two weeks' wages in lieu of notice of termination.

No advance notice of termination or termination pay need be given if an employee is dismissed because of failure to follow company rules, misconduct, or insubordination.

Option #4

Regular work will be provided as far as practicable. However, because of seasonal work loads, there are times when layoffs are necessary. If a layoff should become necessary, employees will be laid off on the basis of their skill, ability, attendance, and production records.

All departments will try to schedule work so that employees who must be laid off can be given adequate advance notice. However, it is recognized that there are times when economic conditions make it impossible to give such advance notice. Every effort will be made to call laid-off employees back to work as soon as possible. An employee who declines recall to his regular job will be considered to have quit.

Option #5

An employee will be subject to discharge only if he cannot, or will not, do satisfactory work after proper instruction and trial, or if his behavior, personal appearance, or attendance are unsatisfactory after three warnings.

An employee will automatically be terminated if he is absent five or more days without reporting to the company within that time with an acceptable explanation for his absence.

Option #6

If an employee quits or is terminated, he automatically loses all seniority and vacation benefits. Should that employee quit and at a later date reapply for work and be accepted, it should be understood that he will be treated like a new employee and will have to start at the lower base rate of pay for his particular job and work to regain seniority.

Additional Notes

The following provision may be added to any of the foregoing options:

If an employee quits or is terminated, he automatically loses all seniority and vacation benefits. Should that employee quit and at a later date reapply for work and be accepted, it should be understood that he will ordinarily be treated as a new employee and will have to start at the lower base rate of pay for his particular job and work to regain seniority.

This may not apply for pension purposes in view of the detailed rules laid down by the new pension law governing both vesting and service.

Timecards

Unless both hourly and salaried employees use the same system, your manual should make clear whether this topic applies to all employees or only to hourly employees. I do not recommend that salaried employees be included within this guideline as there are certain circumstances whereby salaried employees are eligible for comp time. If you opt to make a distinction between employee types make certain that uniformity and fairness are present.

Option #1

It is each employee's obligation to ring his timecard "in" before starting work and "out" at quitting time. No one but a supervisor may ring another person's timecard.

Option #2

Managers will provide each employee with a timecard every pay period. Each day employees are to fill in the total number of hours worked in each job function assigned for that day. (The manager will explain the recording of time by job functions.) Employees must record their own time at the end of each day.

Option #3

All employees are required to punch in at the start of the day, punch out for lunch, punch in after lunch, and punch out at the end of the day. Earnings are calculated from the time shown on the timecard. Any mistakes made should not be corrected by the employee, but the card should be taken to the supervisor for correction with his initials. No one may punch another person's card for him.

Option #4

It is necessary that all hourly employees clock in when entering or leaving the premises for any purposes. This includes the lunch period unless the employee is in the field where time clocks are not accessible.

Here are a few tips about timecards:

1. The time card is the only record for the Payroll Department to use for calculating pay for time worked.

2. It should be kept in its proper place.
3. Another employee's timecard should not be punched, altered, removed, or handled in any way. If another employee's timecard is punched by mistake, the error should be reported to the supervisor immediately.
4. If an employee forgets to clock in or out, the supervisor should be informed immediately.
5. If, for some reason, the supervisor fails to pick up the timecard at the end of the week, he should be notified promptly so the paycheck will be ready on schedule.

Option #5

It is your obligation to ring your timecard "in" before starting work and "out" at quitting time. No one but a supervisor may ring another person's timecard. It is your responsibility to see that the correct time is recorded.

Option #6

Your manager will provide you with a timecard every pay period. Each day you are to fill in the total number of hours worked in each job function assigned to you for that day. Your manager will explain the recording of time by job functions. You must record your own time at the end of each day. Neither the manager or any other employee is permitted to record this time for you.

Option #7

All employees are required to punch in at the start of day, punch out for lunch, punch in after lunch, and punch out at the end of day. Your earnings are calculated from the time shown on the timecard. Make every effort to keep the card clean and legible. Do not correct any mistake; instead, take the card to your supervisor for correction and his initials. No one may punch another's card for him. This can be cause for dismissal for both employees.

CHAPTER 4

GOVERNMENTAL ISSUES

Employee Types

Remember that the traditional distinction between terms of employment for men and women are no longer valid under law. In addition, the 40-hour standard for distinguishing full-time from part-time employment (as suggested in the options) can no longer be used for purposes of pension and profit sharing plans under federal law. If your company has such a plan, you should decide whether to include a note that the 40-hour rule does not apply for purposes of these plans, which contain their own standards, or else substitute the following:

> Regular full-time employee—an employee who customarily works at least 1,000 hours per year. Detailed rules for applying this standard for purposes of the company's [pension] [profit sharing] plan are set forth in the government plan documents.

A similar change would be made in the definition of part-time employment.

Option #1

All employees fall into one of four groups.

1. Probationary Employee—an employee serving the 90-day probationary period, who at the end of successful completion, may become a regular full-time employee. (Such an employee may be terminated without advance notice at any time during the probationary period.)
2. Regular Full-time Employee—an employee who is continuously employed and regularly and customarily works at least 40 hours per week, and who has completed the required probationary period.
3. Part-time Employee—an employee who regularly and customarily works a shorter work week than that of a full-time employee.
4. Temporary Employee—an employee who is employed for a short period of time, usually for a specific purpose, and at the end of which time the need for continued employment no longer exists.

Note: Only regular full-time employees are eligible for company fringe benefits.

Option #2

All employees come under one of the following groups which may be described briefly as follows:

FULL-TIME EMPLOYEES are those who have a regularly scheduled work-week of 40 hours or more and work all year long.

SEASONAL EMPLOYEES are those who work for a short period of time, usually for a specific purpose, and usually for not more than three months.

Employment Policy

You probably don't want a blanket statement saying you will not discriminate on account of age since obviously you will not hire minors who do not meet the child labor rules, and you may desire mandatory retirement policy after age 70. Federal law does prohibit discrimination on account of age with respect to persons between ages 45 and 70. Make sure any ages you do give conform to local law; for instance, some states require non-discrimination against people after age 40. In addition, California and a growing number of other states and local jurisdictions have begun to prohibit discrimination on account of physical or other handicaps, sexual preference, or marital status. This is another reason to check state law before selecting an appropriate policy statement.

Your standard policy on employment should take your needs into consideration for affirmative action. If you employ 50 people or have a $50,000 government contract, you will need a written plan explaining how you intend to increase the number of minorities in your company. You will need the exact EEOC guides for this as there are specific requirements for many segments such as record retention and handicapped personnel.

Option #1

It is the policy of the company to make no discrimination because of sex, color, race, age (between ages 45-70), national origin, or religion in its hiring, promotion, and other employment practices. A new employee will be considered a probationary employee for six (6) months after coming on the payroll. At the end of this period, based upon his demonstrated qualities, a decision will be made as to whether or not an individual will become a permanent employee of the company.

Option #2

It is the policy of the company to adhere to all federal, state, and local guidelines concerning hiring. For further information, contact our personnel department.

Option #3

This company does not allow or condone discrimination in its decision of hiring, promotion, and other employment practices with regards to sex, color, race, age (between ages 45-70), national origin, or religion. In some cases physical, mental, or other mandated certifications will dictate who is qualified to perform certain duties.

Option #4

It is the policy of this company to seek the highest caliber of personal available regardless of sex, color, race, age (between ages 45-70), national origin, or religion.

Note: It is generally a good idea to add a probationary period to any employment policy.

Handicapped

Handicapped personnel can become a great company asset. If you do any business with the government, you could become a privileged vendor by having a positive affirmative action program that seeks out handicapped personnel. Many government procurement bodies have a special set aside program for companies who employ the handicapped. (Large companies are sometimes excluded.) It could become a very important aspect of your company's profitability to avail yourself of these special programs. In some cases you must follow EEOC guidelines.

Option #1

It is a portion of our affirmative action policy that we actively seek out those who are qualified to perform specific work and classified as handicapped.

Option #2

Any employee who meets the federal or state guidelines as handicapped or becomes classified as handicapped should make that fact known for inclusion in their personal records. It is our policy to actively employ the handicapped.

Option #3

It is this firm's policy to meet or exceed all EEOC guidelines for affirmative action. Any qualified applicant who is of a minority or handicapped will receive first consideration for employment where an opening exists.

Option #4

Any applicant who is handicapped will receive prime consideration for any potential employment position if he is deemed qualified to perform the responsibilities necessary.

Harassment

Most employees are sensitive to any kind of treatment by a supervisor that is overbearing. Morale is lost, efficiency is hurt, and long-term attitudes are affected. From these reasons alone, it would behoove most firms to evaluate potential supervisors and other responsible managers as to their views concerning employee relations. (A trend may be emerging in the sending of supervisory personnel to schools specializing in personnel interaction.) Another reason to be concerned is the potential cost of losing a court challenge. Harassment of almost any kind whether mental or sexual is grounds for legal action. A strong statement may assist you in curbing this abuse by your employees and help reduce your risk exposure.

Option #1

Harassment of any person whether another employee or a customer by any member of this firm will be grounds for immediate disciplinary action or dismissal. It is a portion of the agreement of employment that all employees must comply with this policy.

Option #2

This company is determined to set an example in the community and among our peers in the industry, in that harassment of any form will not be tolerated. If you are the target of harassment or if you observe another member of this company harassing anyone, any way, contact a member of management.

Option #3

The current views against harassment of any individual are totally supported by this company. This firm is committed to insuring a pleasant, productive work place free of harassment of almost any kind whether mental, physical, or sexual.

Option #4

The basic belief that all employees deserve the respect and support of their fellow employees is a cornerstone of our demand that we will not allow harassment of any kind whether mental, physical, or sexual to be condoned. Any employee may expect severe disciplinary action or dismissal for breaking this policy.

Hiring Policy

A hiring policy although close is different from an employment policy. Generally hires are thought of as shorter term relationships. Most hires are temporary hourly, piecework, or seasonal workers. They can be placed within the employment policy guidelines as a sub-topic or included into the main statement. However, it is sometimes easier from a legal responsibilities view to make special mention of the separating of the two.

Option #1

Hiring, work assignments, rate of pay, promotions, and layoffs will be based on skill, ability, fitness, length of service, attitude, and quality of work.

Option #2

It is the company's policy to hire all employees on the basis of qualifications, without regard to race, creed, sex, or age.

Option #3

All decisions regarding this company's policy to hire, assign work, pay, promote, lay off will be based on skill, ability, fitness, length of service, attitude, and quality of work.

Option #4

Temporary hires, seasonal, piece workers and contract workers will be selected on the basis qualifications, without regard to race, creed, sex, or age.

Jury Duty

Your company's community responsibility is part of the need to positively encourage employees to honor the legal requirement to jury duty. In doing so, you again have proven the fairness of your firm, and most employees will see the attitude you are striving to project.

That does not mean that you as an employer must suffer due to the loss of a key member of your staff but only that you are encouraging your employees to honor the needs of the community. If you will be negatively impacted by the loss of a key employee at a critical time, some courts will dismiss the employee from service.

Option #1

Employees are encouraged to respond to civic duty when called to serve as a member of a jury panel. Regular full-time employees will receive current daily pay, less any payments received for serving from the city or county. To receive jury duty leave payment, employees should submit the jury summons along with all records of payments received.

Option #2

If called for jury duty, all full-time employees will continue to receive full pay for the days they are required to serve when normally they would be working. All jury duty is computed at eight hours per day straight time. If an employee is called for jury duty but is not required to serve that day, he is expected to return to work.

Option #3

If you are called for jury duty, are selected to serve, and the time off does not create a hardship upon the company, the company will continue your regular pay, less the jury payment, for the duration of your duty. Please notify your department head if you are summoned.

Option #4

You are encouraged to respond to civic duty when called to serve as a member of a jury panel. Regular full-time employees will receive their current daily pay less any payments received for serving from the city or county. To receive your jury duty leave payment, simply submit your jury summons along with all records of payments received.

Option #5

After 90 days of employment, an employee will be excused for jury duty providing his Supervisor is advised immediately upon receipt of notice. The company will pay the difference between jury pay and average straight time earnings.

Option #6

If called upon for jury duty, all full-time employees will continue to receive full pay for the days they are required to serve when they would normally be working. All monies received from court will be endorsed to the company. If you are called upon during a busy season, the company will attempt to have your term delayed until after the busy season. Notify your supervisor immediately upon receipt of jury duty call.

If you report to jury duty but are not required to serve that day, you are expected to return to work. All jury duty pay is computed at eight hours per day straight time.

Option #7

Any regular salaried employee who must serve on jury duty will be paid regular pay with no deductions for time off. The amount paid by the court to the employee will not be deducted from his pay.

Hourly employees will receive pay equivalent to 40 hours work. If the employee works part-time during the week, his pay will still be for 40 hours. If he works more than 40 hours—over and above jury duty time—his pay will be for 40 hours plus any time worked over 40 hours of work—to be paid at rate plus one-half rate (time and a half).

Military Leave

Military leave of absence is a federally mandated requirement for all persons involuntarily entering the armed forces. Many companies have found that the training and discipline that these people receive benefits their work habits and job performance. Therefore, the offer to keep a position open for them upon their return to civilian status is a way to obtain first option on new expertise.

Option #1

All regular, full-time employees will be granted a leave of absence if called for active duty by a branch of the U.S. Armed Services. Every effort will be made to hold open the vacated position at the current rate of pay.

Option #2

If you are drafted into the military service, your rights for reinstatement will be fully protected.

Within 90 days after satisfactorily completing your minimum term of military service, you may apply for reinstatement with the company. If you do not apply within that time, your connection with the company is considered ended. If you decide to return to the company, your military service will be counted as continuous employment in calculating vacation pay and eligibility for the retirement plan. If you were covered by the group insurance or retirement plans at the time you entered military service, the coverage will be reinstated on the first day of your return to work.

Option #3

An employee who returns from service in the Armed Forces of the United States will be reemployed in accordance with whatever law or laws are in effect and which apply in his case. An employee who is a member of a reserve military organization of the United States or of the National Guard, and who attends regular military training camp, will be given necessary time off for such training which will not be considered vacation time. After 90 days of employment, the company will supplement the difference (if any) of training pay and average earnings. Immediately upon notice of scheduled time of training, your supervisor is to be advised.

Worker's Compensation

Workman's Compensation is normally regulated on a local level. Even though there are examples below, it is strongly suggested that you check with your local governing authority to make sure the wording and content of your statement and its compliance with local regulations.

Option #1

Workman's Compensation insurance is provided by the company as required by state law. It provides employees with payments for any injury resulting from an accident while working for the company. Payments begin after the seventh day of total disability. The insurance company names certain doctors to whom an employee must go in order to receive payment under this insurance.

During the period of recovery from a temporary injury, employees will receive payments from the insurance company. These payments will continue until the doctor releases the employee to return to work. If the type of injury requires a period of convalescence, the company will grant a 90-day period before the employee is required to return to work. Regardless of the type of injury, it must be reported promptly and properly.

Option #2

All employees must be sure to report promptly to their section heads in full detail all accidents or injuries. If they are injured on the job, they are covered by insurance and entitled to compensation in accordance with the Workers' Compensation Law.

CHAPTER 5

EMPLOYEE BENEFIT ISSUES

Education Opportunities

In aggressive companies, it is common for continuing education programs to be offered to employees, either in an effort to keep their personnel up to date on the latest knowledge or as a competitive edge in recruiting top talent.

The use of any benefit must be uniform and apply to all employees. It would look strange to the IRS, if all six of your children went to a fine college on the educational package your firm offers, especially if the rest of your employees were not made aware of these opportunities.

Option #1

This is a young and growing company. We have room for advancement within the ranks, and we will continue to have as the company grows. We will do everything we can to encourage you, not only to learn your job, but to learn other parts of the operation and other jobs as well.

As our company grows, so will employee benefits, it is wise to remember that you are not only working for the company but also for yourself.

You will find that the more you learn and the better you are able to function in your job, the more money you will make and the faster you will advance with us. You will be exposed to regular on-the-job training sessions and voluntary sessions as well. The more interest you show on your job, the faster you will advance.

We have instituted a basic training program for new employees as well as a continual on-the-job training of all employees.

Option #2

Your future is dependent on the effort put forth physically and mentally to better qualify yourself and to insure your future. For any employee completing an approved course of education in a period of two years, we will pay for the course at completion.

Option #3

Knowledge is an important key to success here. Each division schedules and conducts training meetings to fill the needs of its people. In addition, general meetings for everyone in the organization are held from time to time.

We want you to grow with the company, and we will help you in every way.

Option #4

An employee wishing to improve his knowledge in areas related to employment with the company is encouraged to enroll in such educational courses at community colleges or short courses that may be offered. The company will pay the tuition fee, at an approved school, for courses which are approved by the manager, providing the employee satisfactorily completes the course.

Employee Purchase Discounts

It is normally to your company's benefit to encourage employees to gain confidence in company products by using them. A side benefit is the employee's ability to more fully explain product functions from a personal point of view. Sometimes after an employee has used a product, he may see additional uses or improvements that can prove profitable to your company. In addition, allowing employee purchase discounts often contributes to high company morale. Thus, you may want to establish a policy concerning employee purchase discounts.

Option #1

Permanent employees are entitled to a 40% discount off the sales price of items produced by the company, and 20% off other items sold through the company. Please note that items bought at discount prices are for personal use or for gifts only.

Option #2

After 30 days of employment, employees may purchase merchandise from the company for their home or as occasional gifts at 20% under the current wholesale price, plus sales tax.

Option #3

All employees will receive a 20% discount on any item sold by the company. The only exception will be items marked down for quick sale.

Option #4

As a permanent employee of the company, you are entitled to 40% discount off the retail price of items sold by the company. Please note that items bought at discount prices are for your personal use or for gifts only.

Option #5

The company has earned the reputation of having excellent merchandise. People come from miles away to purchase our products. With the following guidelines, your company wishes to offer you the opportunity to purchase at a discount. The employee will:

1. Be employed for three months.
2. Make selections on his own time.
3. Make selections for his own personal use only.
4. Pay for purchases in cash or by payroll deduction at the first payroll period following purchase.
5. Secure approval for purchases from your Store Manager/Supervisor.

Discount Percentages:
40% off retail

Option #6

Purchases may be made from the company at 20% discount from their regular price. You will pay for items by cash or through payroll deductions, within the two following pay periods after purchases. All purchases are handled in the regular company billing procedure. You are subject to state sales tax. Purchases of excessive amounts will be checked.

Option #7

All regular full-time and regular part-time employees are eligible for employee discount privileges at any of our stores. You will receive an employee discount and credit card which you may use to shop for merchandise for your own personal use.

During any off-duty time, present your card and have your purchase authorized by the store manager or assistant manager. All employee discount purchases must be charged, and your discount will be allowed on payment of your account on or before the due date.

The merchandise must be for your own use and benefit and may not be purchased at discount for any other party.

Option #8

Upon completion of thirty (30) days employment, all employees are eligible to receive discount privileges as follows:

Twenty percent discount on all purchases.

All purchases must be paid in full by the tenth day of the month following purchase. Failure to pay in full will result in the loss of the discount and interest to be charged at the rate of 1 1/2% per month which is an annual charge of 18%.

Every employee discount purchase must be written up on a sales invoice by a fellow employee and charged to the employee making the purchase. (No cash sales.)

Employee discounts are allowable only on merchandise to be used by the employee for his own benefit. Under no circumstances will merchandise be purchased for other parties with these discounts. An employee automatically forfeits discount privileges if above policy is violated.

Option #9

Each employee may purchase any product from the company on a cash basis at a substantial discount. Any such requests are to be channeled through either the General Manager or Supervisor. Payment for products bought must be paid for the same week bought. Purchases by an employee are to be limited to $100 a year per employee.

Funeral Leave

Prior to the time that an employee has an occasion when he wishes to attend a funeral, he should have received guidelines that will help him put his needs and the company's needs in perspective.

Although the possibility does exist for abuse of this policy, it is not recognized by personal departments as one of the areas chronically used as an excuse for absenteeism.

Option #1

Regular, full-time employees are allowed up to three days of paid funeral leave to arrange for and attend the funeral of a member of his or her immediate family.

Option #2

In the event of a death in your immediate family (father, mother, spouse, children, sister, or brother), the company will pay you for up to five days, leave. You must obtain authorization in advance from your department head.

Option #3

If a death occurs in an employee's immediate family, the employee will be paid for eight hours work, at his regular base rate for two consecutive days while making funeral arrangements and attending the funeral. Supervisors should be notified immediately.

Option #4

Leave time for a funeral not of the employee's immediate family may be considered as vacation days if approved in advance by your supervisor. If an employee has not earned vacation time, he may discuss with his supervisor the possibility of unpaid leave.

Holidays

Many holidays can work to your benefit if approached correctly and announced well in advance of their occurrence. Special events, such as picnics, can be planned or special marketing plans enacted. However, it is equally important that you plan a sale or inventory to occur during this time to provide a way either to compensate the employees or to provide an alternate day off.

Option #1

There are six paid holidays each year. They are New Year's Day, Memorial Day, July 4th, Labor Day, Thanksgiving, and Christmas. To be eligible for holiday pay, you must be a regular, full-time employee. A regular, full-time employee is one who has been in the company's employ full-time for three or more months.

Option #2

Regular, full-time employees will receive the following holidays with pay providing they work their regularly scheduled workday before and workday after the holiday:

New Year's Day - January 1
Independence Day - July 4
Memorial Day - Last Monday in May
Labor Day - First Monday in September
Thanksgiving Day - Fourth Thursday in November
Christmas Day - December 25

Holiday pay is computed at the employee's regular rate of pay and is not included as time worked. Although all divisions are closed on Easter Sunday, this is not a paid holiday.

Option #3

Ordinarily, business operations will be suspended in observance of New Year's Day, Memorial Day, July 4th, Labor Day, Thanksgiving, and Christmas. When the holiday falls on Sunday, the following Monday is considered a holiday and the business will remain closed.

Option #4

Each full-time regular employee, after one year's service, who worked the full scheduled workday before, and the full scheduled workday after a holiday will be paid eight hours at his straight time hourly rate for each holiday as follows: New Year's Day, Memorial Day, July 4th, Labor Day, Thanksgiving, and Christmas.

Option #5

New Year's, Memorial, Independence, Labor, Thanksgiving, and Christmas days are paid holidays for all full-time permanent employees. When a holiday falls on a Saturday, the preceding Friday will be considered a holiday; when it falls on a Sunday, the following Monday will be considered a holiday. When a holiday falls within your vacation period, an additional day will be added to your vacation.

Option #6

Full-time employees receive the following paid holidays:

New Year's Day
Memorial Day
Independence Day
Labor Day
Thanksgiving Day
Christmas Day
(Other/Birthday)

An employee must have worked for 12 months before becoming eligible for paid holidays. All paid holidays will be computed on the basis of an eight-hour day. Each employee must report to work each working day the week previous to the holiday and the first working day after the holiday to receive pay for that holiday.

Seasonal employees who have worked the entire previous season will be eligible for any of the applicable holidays which fall within their term of seasonal employment. Other rules for eligibility are the same as those for full-time employees.

In the event that a holiday falls on a Saturday, the preceding Friday will be designated as a holiday. If a holiday falls on Sunday, the following Monday will be designated as a holiday.

Option #7

Paid holidays include New Year's Day, Memorial Day, July 4th, Labor Day, Thanksgiving Day, (Other), and Christmas. Eight hours' pay will be given for any full-time employee providing he works one full workday either before or after the holiday, except if weather interferes or if he is on vacation.

Option #8

Except for special work, no work will be performed on the following holidays or days on which they are observed:

New Year's Day
Memorial Day
Independence Day
Labor Day
Thanksgiving Day
Christmas Day
(Other)

These will be paid holidays to all full-time employees having one year or more with the company; however, to be paid for the holidays, an employee must have worked the workday preceding and the workday following each holiday.

These six paid holidays are equivalent to one extra week's vacation each year.

Insurance Programs

The legal requirements dictating the manner in which details of this benefit must be explained makes it much more practical to make available a separate document based on your specific insurance program rather than attempt to summarize or explain it in a publication such as your policy manual.

Option #1

An attractive insurance program has been adopted by the company for the benefit of employees. Full details are provided in a separate document.

Option #2

Group Health and Major Medical

Regular, full-time employees are covered under the Company Basic Health Plan and the Company Major Medical Plan. Your premiums will be paid monthly by the Company. You may include your dependents by making arrangements with the personnel manager in the administrative office. Premiums for dependent coverage will be deducted monthly from your paycheck. Your coverage under these health plans is evidenced by a Health Insurance Membership Card along with booklets describing the basic plan benefits and the major plan benefits.

Option #3

The company is contracted now with the Jones Insurance Company for a complete hospital and medical plan, as well as life insurance, with double indemnity clause. You are invited to take part in this program after you have been employed for a period of 90 days. The company pays one-half of the cost; the balance is a payroll deduction.

Option #4

Group life, health, and accident insurance plans are offered to you as part of the company's benefit program. You are eligible to participate in the insurance program after you have completed three months' employment if you are a full-time employee. The company will pay the entire premium on your personal insurance. Dependent coverage is available to you at the rate charged by the insurance company (our cost), if desired, with the premium deducted from your pay check.

Option #5

Upon completion of three months' continuous full-time service, an employee will become eligible for major medical insurance coverage as follows:

$15,000 Major Medical Insurance Policy from Jones Accident and Life Insurance Company.

The company will pay 100% of employee's share as long as employee works full-time.

Employees may, at their own expense, include their dependents on the plan at the regular group rates. All employees are encouraged to take advantage of the lower rates offered to this group.

Overtime

Unless you pay overtime to all employees, including exempt agricultural and management/professional employees, you should use the term nonexempt in describing the group eligible for premium overtime. It is also important to have the Wage and Hour Board rules handy. Some states do not allow the paying of overtime an option, though federal regulations have certain flexibilities.

Option #1

You will not be requested to work overtime except in case of need during peak seasons. When it is known that overtime work cannot be avoided, every effort will be made to advise you at least 24 hours in advance. In those instances, employees eligible for overtime will receive one and one-half times their regular pay after working 40 hours of straight time in any one week.

Option #2

Overtime will be worked only when absolutely necessary, and employees are expected to work necessary overtime. Overtime work will be distributed as equitably as practical among those qualified to do the work on a production basis. Overtime pay is one and one-half times the basic straight time hourly rate (average straight time hourly earnings for incentive workers) and will be paid for all hours worked over 40 in a regular work week.

Option #3

You are paid one and one-half times your regular hourly rate for all work in any week over 40 hours. Saturday and/or Sunday work pays one and one-half times your regular rate only after you have worked 40 hours in that week. If at any time you should work on a paid holiday, you will receive your holiday pay for that day and your regular pay at one and one-half times your regular rate provided you have worked 40 hours or more in that week; otherwise, you will be paid at your regular rate.

Option #4

Employees covered by the wage-hour laws are paid for overtime hours in excess of 40 hours per week at a rate of one and one-half times their regular rate. In addition, if they work on a paid holiday, they are entitled to holiday pay. Exempt hourly employees are paid for such overtime at their regular hourly rate and are also entitled to holiday pay if they work on a paid holiday. Exempt salaried employees are expected to work whatever overtime may be required, including any holidays, without additional compensation.

Option #5

Employees covered by the wage-hour laws are paid for overtime hours in excess of 40 hours per week at a rate of one and one-half times their regular rate. In addition, if employees work on a paid holiday, they are entitled to holiday pay. Exempt hourly employees are paid at their regular rate for hours over 40 per week. In addition, employees are entitled to holiday pay for working on a paid holiday, if at least 40 hours have been worked in that week. Exempt salaried employees are expected to work whatever overtime may be required, including any holidays, without additional compensation.

Option #6

Employees covered by the wage-hour laws are paid for overtime hours in excess of 40 hours per week at a rate of one and one-half times their regular rate. They are also entitled to premium overtime for any hours worked on Saturdays or Sundays. In addition, if they work on a paid holiday, they are entitled to holiday pay. Exempt hourly employees are paid for such overtime at their regular hourly rate and are also entitled to holiday pay if they work on a paid holiday. Exempt salaried employees are expected to work whatever overtime may be required, including any holidays, without additional compensation.

Option #7

Employees covered by the wage-hour laws are paid for overtime hours in excess of 40 hours per week at a rate of one and one-half times their regular rate. In addition, if they work on a paid holiday, they are entitled to holiday pay. Exempt hourly employees are paid at their regular rate for hours over 40 per week. In addition, they are entitled to holiday pay for working on a paid holiday if at least 40 hours have been worked in that week. Exempt salaried employees are expected to work whatever overtime may be required, including any holidays, without additional compensation. Overtime will be worked only when absolutely necessary, and employees are expected to work necessary overtime.

Maternity and Paternity Leave

Paternity leave is a fairly new concept arising out of the equal rights awareness activity. You may not be prepared for it, but you may be able to handle it better if you consider the ways it could be handled.

Your company probably has certain criteria that govern maternity leave and it may be construed as a sexual discrimination if you do allow these same allowances for paternity leave.

In general the company should consider that parenthood affects both the mother and the father. (Notice that I did not use the terms husband or wife: these are not pertinent to the issue of paternity leave nor for that case to maternity leave.) Therefore, unless you wish to test the validly of the law, do not make allowances for the mother that differ from those offered to the father.

In general, leave of absence for childbirth is granted to employees based upon the amount of time that the employee has worked for the organization.

A similar policy might be considered in adoption circumstances. Although not a common an occurrence, a company that shows this kind of progressive attitude would show employees where their concerns are located.

Option #1

A leave of absence is granted to all employees for child bearing reasons, based upon individual needs. You must provide a written notification from the attending physician for verification purposes. The company allows one weeks' paid leave for each full year of employment, up to three weeks. Maximum time off for child bearing is six weeks. If your time off exceeds six weeks, the company will make an effort to offer you a position in a similar situation if available.

Pay Period

In most states pay periods have some flexibility but are defined by law under the Board of Labor. You should ascertain that your pay policy is within applicable guidelines. Some states have started adopting requirements for prompt pay of employees normally excluded (such as contract and commission employees) with penalties for failure to comply.

Option #1

The pay period begins on Thursday of each week and ends on Wednesday. Payday is on a weekly basis on Friday. Checks are available at the completion of your workday and cover time worked in the preceding Thursday through Wednesday period.

Option #2

The company pays employees on a biweekly basis on Saturday (every other week). Salary advances are not permitted. You are encouraged to bank your checks promptly. Payroll checks may not be cashed at the company.

Option #3

The pay period is two full weeks, the last day closing on a Saturday. Paychecks are issued the following week on the third regular workday of that week.

Option #4

Paychecks will be distributed every Friday. Any questions about your paycheck may be taken up with the Supervisor. If payday falls on a holiday, checks will be distributed on the day before.

Option #5

The payroll period for all employees starts from the opening of business on Tuesday to the close of business on the following Monday. Paychecks are processed by a computer system and are attached to your timecard at the close of your workday on Friday of each week. No advances in pay are permitted.

Option #6

Hourly employees are paid every two weeks on Friday for all work performed in the two-week period ending the preceding Saturday.

Salaried employees are paid semimonthly on the 5th and 20th for work performed in the first and second half of the month. If payday falls on a Saturday, Sunday, employees are paid on the preceding Friday. If payday falls on a holiday, employees are paid on the preceding day.

Option #7

The pay period for hourly employees begins on Thursday of each week and ends on Wednesday. Payday is on a weekly basis on Friday. Checks are available at the completion of the workday, covering time worked in the preceding Thursday through Wednesday period.

Salaried employees are paid on the 15th and last day of each month for a semimonthly pay period ending on that day.

Option #8

Supervisors will distribute paychecks each Wednesday after 4:00 p.m. for the pay period which closed the previous Saturday night. If an employee is absent on the regular payday, the check will be returned to the Payroll Department to be held for the employee's return unless it is to be mailed. If the paycheck is to be picked up by another person, a written request must be presented to the Supervisor, signed and dated by the person making the request.

Profit Sharing

The legal requirements dictating the manner in which details of this benefit must be explained makes it much more practical to make available a separate document based on your specific profit sharing plan rather than attempt to summarize or explain it in a policy manual.

Option #1

A profit sharing plan has been adopted by the company for the benefit of the employees. Full details are provided in a separate document.

Option #2

All regular, full-time employees with at least one calendar year of continuous service are qualified to participate in the Company Employee's Profit Sharing Plan. When the company has a good, profitable year, all participants share in the success through the Profit Sharing Plan. It's an incentive for everyone to pull together to get the job done.

Your first full calendar year of continuous employment as a regular, full-time employee is your qualifying year for the Profit Sharing Plan.

Your second full calendar year as a regular, full-time employee is your first participating year.

You will be invited to the annual meeting of participants in the Company Employee's Profit Sharing Plan during the early part of your third full calendar year, where you will receive a certificate telling you the amount of Profit Sharing funds allocated to your account.

Our company builds for your future security through this plan; you can make an important contribution to the success of the plan by working for the success of the company.

Option #3

A profit sharing plan has been adopted by the company for the benefit of the employees. All regular, full-time employees who have completed one year's continuous service are entitled to participate in the plan. All contributions to the plan will be made by the company from the company profits and allocated to the participants on the basis of annual compensation and length of service. The larger the profits of the company, the greater the contribution that will be made to the profit sharing fund.

Benefits are paid on account of death, disability, or retirement. If your employment terminates for any reason after the completion of two years' service, you are entitled to a portion of your profit sharing account as follows:

2 years - 10%
3 years - 20%
4 years - 40%
5 years - 60%
6 years - 80%
7 years - 100%

Retirement Plan

The legal requirements dictating the manner in which details of this benefit must be explained makes it much more practical to make available a separate document based on your specific retirement program rather than attempt to summarize or explain it in a publication as this.

In considering a retirement plan, check your records to determine the percentage of employees that may be affected within five years and seek them out. The information and feedback those employees can provide will be invaluable. Often companies find it advantageous to offer retirees a more flexible working hours program, thereby keeping experience on line and allowing the retiree to continue to be a productive member of our community.

Option #1

The company has established a retirement program for the benefit of employees. Full details are provided in a separate document.

Option #2

You will become eligible to join the company retirement plan after you have completed two years of continuous service provided you have not attained your 65th birthday.

The plan is a cooperative one which calls for contributions from both you and the company. Your contributions will be based on your earnings, and the company will contribute approximately twice the amount contributed by members.

Although 65 is the normal retirement age, earlier retirements may be arranged under certain conditions.

You will be notified when you become eligible to join and will be given a booklet explaining the retirement plan in detail.

Option #3

All employees are eligible for United States Social Security, Age Retirement Benefits are available after employment for a sufficient period of time. You become eligible at age 62 or any time thereafter. Information about Social Security may be obtained from your supervisor, or he can tell you where to find the information if he does not know. Because the company contributes to the Social Security program for you, there is no other retirement fund. There is no set retirement age.

Savings Plan

Savings plans are not a hot item on most companies' agenda, but they are still viable if you wish to show your employees that you are interested in their well-being. Because many rules and regulations focus on this benefit, you should seek specialized assistance if you decide to go the extra mile for your employees.

Option #1

A savings plan is operated by the company for the convenience and benefit of the employees.

Upon written instruction, the company will deduct money from an employee's wages and deposit it in his account at any branch of [NAME OF BANK].

This deduction is made from the paycheck designated by the employee, and the funds withheld represent a savings account which may be withdrawn by the employee at any time. Funds accumulated in such a savings account may be useful for the payment of federal income taxes; however, laws also permit the company to make voluntary federal income tax withholding for those employees requesting it, including in cases where tax withholding is not required.

Severance Pay

Severance pay is occasionally used in lieu of notice. It is a normally accepted business need for employees to give notice of their intent to leave, and business often returns the favor by allowing severance pay when terminating an employee.

When deciding on your firm's position, consider whether to include all employees, full-time employees, salaried employees, seasonal employees, and/or part-time employees. Also you may wish to allow yourself some latitude in how or to whom severance pay is given.

Option #1

In certain cases when lack of work or other cause necessitates the termination of an employee, the company will give two weeks' pay in lieu of notice.

Option #2

When lack of work causes the termination of an employee, and providing the employee has had good performance reviews over the last two reviews, the company will provide two weeks' severance in lieu of notice.

Option #3

At the discretion of the company, severance pay equal to one week for each year of employment will be provided to discharged employees.

Sick Leave

If you have insurance—whether for short-term or long-term disability—it is important that your policy regarding sick leave be consistent with your coverage. You might find it more desirable to summarize your sick leave insurance policy briefly and refer employees to a separate brochure or to you for details. Note that under present federal law, pregnancy may be treated like any other disability.

Option #1

All full-time employees (40 hours or more per week—hourly or salaried) will accrue sick leave at the following rates:

One-half day leave for each full month of continued employment, with a maximum of six days' credit in any one year.

All sick leave pay is computed at eight hours per day straight time. Sick leave credit is not accumulative and cannot be carried over to the following year.

Option #2

Regular, full-time employees are eligible for sick leave with pay according to this schedule:

- Under six months service—None
- Over six months up to one calendar year of continuous regular full time service—five days
- Each additional calendar year of continuous regular full-time service—five additional days.

Sick pay credits not used may be carried forward and accumulated from year to year up to a maximum of ten weeks (50 days).

Option #3

After 90 days of employment, you can accumulate one-half day per month to be used for personal illness only. However, sick leave is cumulative so that long-time employees can accumulate time in case of major illness. Sick leave is given for illness only+a doctor's verification may be required. Should your employment terminate, unused sick leave will not be paid since it is for illness only.

Option #4

After two years of continuous service (excepting leave of absence time) and upon the written verification of a recognized medical doctor, you will be paid at your regular hourly rate for your absence due to a illness commencing with the sixth working day of absence thereafter. For purposes of computing this payment, a working day is eight hours and is any day Monday through Friday.

Option #5

All full-time personnel who have at least 90 days of continuous service are eligible for ten days of paid sick leave per year. Any employee who uses or requires more than ten days sick leave per year will receive no pay for those taken in excess of the ten days allotted. In the event that it is necessary to take a sick day, all employees are asked to call in at 8:00 a.m. Sick days are counted from June 1st to May 31st each year.

Option #6

If an employee is injured or becomes ill, he is expected to notify the company immediately, or if he is too ill, to see that someone else notifies the company. The company will grant sick leave without pay in all cases of bona fide illness. If the employee is absent for one week or more, a note from the doctor attesting to the injury or illness and the total time the employee may be absent from work may be required.

Suggestion Awards

Employees appreciate special recognition and, when encouraged, become adept at spotting possible improvements or cost saving measures. An awards program could be one of the most profitable areas any company could enact. Many employees have a hunch or idea that could be stunning to the profitability of your company, but if they do not feel that they are encouraged to speak out, they will not!

Even suggestions that produce little compensation to your company can promote your progressive attitudes in the market place.

Option #1

A Suggestion Awards Committee handles the suggestion awards program within the company. The committee meets every month and evaluates employee suggestions submitted during the month for suggestions worthy of an award. The awards are $15, $10, and $5. In addition, annual awards of $100, $50, and $25 are given for the first, second, and third place suggestions during the previous year.

Employees are encouraged to be alert for labor-saving or safety suggestions. Many improvements in the company's operation have resulted from suggestions made by employees. Supervisors will help prepare suggestions employees propose for submission.

Option #2

The company is constantly searching for new and better ways to improve productivity and profits. Suggestion boxes are located in several areas to assist employees in sharing their ideas. The employee submitting the best idea for cutting costs or improving productivity each season will receive a cash prize of $50. Each employee who submits an idea that is used will receive a cash prize of $10.

Vacations

Although not required by law most companies provide for some form of vacation in their policy. Factors to consider in making a vacation policy include:

1. The length of service required before becoming eligible for vacation time.
2. The amount of vacation time given after that length of service.
3. The months in which vacation may be taken.
4. Whether vacation benefits may be carried forward and for how long.
5. Whether terminating employees would be paid for unused vacation time. (Note that the law in some states, including California, now requires such payment.)
6. Whether all vacation time must be taken consecutively or may be taken in smaller units such as a week, a day, or an hour.

Option #1

After one year of continuous employment, you will be entitled to one week of vacation subsequent to the anniversary of your hiring date. After two years of employment, you are entitled to two weeks of vacation each year. After ten years of continuous service, you will be entitled to three weeks of vacation each year. All vacations must be taken by December 31 of the calendar year in which the anniversary of your hiring date falls.

Option #2

Each full-time employee with at least one year, but less than three years of continuous service with the company, will be entitled to one week of vacation with pay. Full-time employees with more than three and up to ten years of service, is entitled to two weeks vacation with pay. With more than ten years of service, full-time employees are eligible for three weeks of vacation with pay. Employees will, within specified months, be permitted to take their vacation at the time they request. However, all vacation dates must be approved by their supervisor. Employees with over two weeks' vacation entitlement will be allowed two weeks in July or August and the remainder in January or February.

Option #3

All full-time personnel who have completed six months of continuous service are eligible for one week paid vacation. After one year's continuous service, each employee covered will be eligible for two weeks' paid vacation. Vacations are to be scheduled anytime during the summer months but are subject to approval by the General Manager. In cases where two or more employees of the same department desire the same vacation dates, seniority will prevail. Vacation pay will be calculated on the basis of your regular weekly pay and will be paid on the Friday you leave for vacation.

Option #4

Regular full-time employees will receive vacations with pay at the regular rate according to this schedule.

If you were hired before:	You will receive these days of vacation with pay:
March 1 this year	2 days
January 1 this year	3 days
November 1 last year	4 days
September 1 last year	5 days
January 1 last year	6 days
January 1 two years ago	7 days
January 1 three years ago	8 days
January 1 four years ago	9 days
January 1 five years ago	10 days = 2 weeks

Option #5

Hourly Employees: (a) one week of paid vacation after one year's employment based on 1/52 of previous fifty-two weeks' hours times weekly rate at time of vacation, or those employees not having completed fifty-two weeks, but more than twenty-six weeks, will receive a pro rata of 1/26 weeks; (b) two weeks' after two years.

Salaried Employees: (a) one week paid vacation after one year's employment, or if eligible, after six months; (b) two weeks after two years.

Commissioned Employees: Same as above. Weekly vacation pay based on 1/52 of previous total commissions paid for each week.

If a person starts prior to March 1 and works six months, he is entitled to one week's vacation. Those starting after March 1 must wait until 12 months have passed to receive one week's vacation. July 1 is the earliest date that a vacation can be taken, and all vacations must be taken by February 1 of the following year.

Employees will not be paid for unused vacation time when resigning. Vacations cannot be carried over to the next vacation period.

Option #6

Full-time employees will receive one week of paid vacation after one year of employment and two weeks after ten years of continuous employment. Vacations will be based on a 40-hour work week. Full-time employees should make arrangements with their supervisor to schedule vacations several weeks in advance to insure proper staffing during busy production seasons.

Seasonal employees, at the end of their second season of employment, will receive eight hours' paid vacation for each 400 hours worked, up to a maximum of 40 hours' paid vacation.

Part-time employees are not eligible for paid vacations.

Option #7

- One week (40 hours) after one year.
- Two weeks after three years.
- Three weeks after 15 years.
- Fractions paid on a pro rata basis after the first year.

Note: *Provisions which may be added to any of the foregoing options:*

- Employees are encouraged to schedule their vacations during off-season periods.
- Vacations should ordinarily be taken each year in full. However, the unused vacation credits accruing in prior years may be carried forward past the end of a year only to the extent that the total carried forward does not exceed one-half of the total credits accrued during the year just ended. (Exceptions by special advance arrangement only.)
- Unused vacation time will not be paid for, except that terminating employees may be paid for vacation time accrued during the current year and any vacation time carried forward from prior pay periods in accordance with the policy stated above.
- Vacation times shall be taken in increments of [full work days] [half days] [hours].

Wage and Salary Advances

The issue of wage and salary advances is a sensitive topic to say the least. You do not want to be taken advantage of, yet under some humane circumstances it maybe to the company's benefit to help an employee in need. You must weigh the potential good will and gratitude generated by the amount of risk exposure. Whatever you decide, it would be prudent to address this topic ahead of time. Also, it is not wise to charge interest due to usury regulations and laws.

Option #1

Wage or salary advances can be permitted in rare situations, on sufficient advance notice, in case of emergency or unusual hardship. In addition, salary or wages falling due during scheduled vacation periods will be payable on the last working day before the vacation.

Option #2

No wage or salary advances are permitted.

Option #3

In rare circumstances of extreme hardship, salary advances are permitted in amounts of up to 50% of average weekly earnings. Repayment will be deducted from earnings over the next four (4) pay periods.

Option #4

Requests for wage and salary advances must be submitted to your supervisor for consideration. If approved, an amount of up to of 25% of estimated normal monthly income will be considered. Repayment will be deducted over the next four (4) pay periods.

Working Hours

One of the easier ways to make an unintentional breach of the labor board is to not give consideration and study to the existing regulations concerning work rules in your particular area. Employers who have not done this homework, have paid back wages and been assessed fines that could have been prevented with proper research.

Generally, in the case of a nonexempt hourly employee, labor laws require that such employees be paid for not only time actually worked, but also time required for preparation and cleanup, and (to the extent paid for by customer, practice, or contract) transportation between the location to which the employee reports and any remote location where the work is conducted. In addition, in case of out-of-town travel, such an employee should be paid for travel time (other than local commuting to his employer's premises) and for time either worked or on call at the out-of-town location. As an exception, the employee need not be paid for travel time outside of normal working hours (including the same hours on weekends and holidays).

The work week may be any consecutive period of seven twenty-four hour periods, although it usually begins at 00:01 a.m. on Sunday or Monday. The scheduled work hours should be 40 hours or fewer; otherwise, refer to the section on overtime. Any difference in the normal working hours for men and for women is a basis for a claim of sex discrimination.

Option #1

The basic workday is eight hours, and the basic work week is 40 hours. Your own hours of work will depend on the needs of the department to which you are assigned. Instructions regarding scheduled days of work and starting and quitting times will be explained by your supervisor.

Option #2

Regular working hours are from 8:00 a.m. to 5:00 p.m., Monday through Friday. Lunch hour is from 12:00 p.m. to 1:00 p.m. Extra hours and Saturday work are scheduled as necessary during the busy times of the year.

You are expected to be at your assigned place of work at the scheduled time to begin work.

The company provides transportation for Production Department employees to the assigned work place.

Option #3

Your supervisor will inform you of your working hours, which will vary according to season and job.

Option #4

The workday begins at 8:00 a.m. the year round; on occasion you might be asked to report earlier for a special reason. Quitting time will vary according to the season. Your foreman will inform you of the time changes.

CHAPTER 6

CUSTOMER ISSUES

Check Acceptance

Although your company may not be engaged in retail sales and does not consider a check cashing policy necessary you may want to reconsider, as there are occasions when your employees may find using the petty cash fund for the purpose of quick cash more convenient than leaving work to go to a bank.

If your company is involved in retail or processes a volume of checks you will most certainly wish to consider establishing some form of policy concerning checks. It would be advisable to consult with the local prosecuting attorney to obtain specific procedures needed to allow him to collect on bad paper, since if you accept checks, then eventually you will get a worthless piece of paper.

You may wish to allow some flexibility in your policy by the use of words such as generally and good judgment, but this is one of those sensitive areas where your personnel may become overly protective of the company and unintentionally create bad public relations You might wish to avoid that situation by checking the reactions of your employees and if surprised by their responses, then soften the attitudes expressed while complimenting their loyalty.

Option #1

The company accepts approved checks in payment of invoices it may issue. When the writer or endorser of a check is a new customer, normal identification procedures will be followed. By "normal identification procedures" is meant the requesting of the customer to show a state issued ID card with picture or driver's license and a major credit card. The company generally will not cash checks when no purchase is made.

Option #2

It is this company's policy to accept approved checks from our customers. Any clerk receiving checks in payment should assure himself the person issuing the check is as presented. If the customer is not personally known, ask to see a driver's license and then copy driver's license number and customers address, phone number, and place of employment on the back of the check. Mark on sales slip "paid by check #____." Clerk should place his initials on the left-hand corner of the front of the check.

Option #3

The company does not accept personal checks and will accept company checks only with the approval of our credit department. Otherwise, only cash, credit cards, money orders, and cashier's checks are acceptable.

Option #4

This company will accept checks for amount of purchase only and then only with acceptable identification and major credit card.

Customer Accident/Injury

You have probably seen signs in various businesses stating "We are not responsible for accidents." This type of disclaimer is almost always considered invalid especially if there was a reasonable expectation that an accident could have been prevented by reasonable actions.

The purpose of this book is not to propose risk management actions but to help you and your employees to reduce the amount of your exposure if an accident occurs. It seems certain that an accident victim will note the actions you take to ease his or her pain or relive tensions, with a possible result that the victim may not wish to go to court.

Option #1

In the event of a accident involving a customer, find out if the customer wants or needs medical assistance to be called or if he will seek out his own remedy. If the damage is severe call the emergency medical service and make the customer as comfortable as possible while waiting. According to severity, it may not be wise to move the injured person, especially if the head neck or spine is involved. If the injury is minor be helpful and supportive. *Do not volunteer statements such as "we have needed to get that step fixed for six months."*

After the customer has left, write a sequence of events listing - time, where, who, what happened, what you observed of the customer, appearance of the customer, sobriety, and any other circumstances that you noticed. *Then call your area manager or home office.*

Option #2

We are concerned with how well our customers think of our company. In obtaining the goodwill of the public we believe that any good we can do for our fellow man is not lost.

If a customer has an accident on our premises, we want to offer whatever aid possible. *Use good judgment!* Always think before acting. It is imperative to remember the axiom "Cause no harm." Unless you are certain that it will not cause further injury, *Do not move an accident victim,* unless you believe not moving them will allow greater injury to happen. If an injury is minor, be helpful and supportive. *Do not volunteer statements like "we have needed to get that step fixed for six months."*

After the customer has left, write a sequence of events that lists - time, where, who, what happened, what you observed of the customer, appearance of the customer, sobriety, and any other circumstances that you noticed. *Then notify your manager and home office.*

Option #3

In the event of a accident involving a customer who is conscious, find out if the customer wants or needs medical assistance to be called. If the damage is severe or if the victim is unconscious, call the emergency medical service and make the customer as comfortable as possible while waiting. At all times be supportive and speak positively about the injury. Do not cause tension to increase. Think before speaking. Do not make any statements you feel should be addressed by our legal consul. After the customer has left, write a sequence of events that lists - time, where, who, what happened, what you observed of the customer, appearance of the customer, sobriety, and any other circumstances that you noticed. *Then notify your manager and home office .*

Option #4

In the event of any accident, no matter whose fault, even if the customer says don't worry, all employees are required to write an incident report. Start making mental notes of what you see or hear, what the conditions are, what the customer was doing, etc. No matter how small your remembrance of the event is, it could tell all the information that is normally forgotten unless written immediately. Basic first aid is to call for emergency medical assistance. *Do not move an accident victim.* Offer support and caring until emergency medical assistance arrives.

Customer Complaints

Since customers are the lifeblood of your company, you cannot afford to neglect customer complaints. The manner in which your employees respond to a customer's complaint to a large extent reflects how they perceive the "official" attitude of your company. That single observation should be reason enough for you to set the tone of your employees' response with a well-chosen statement of policy.

First, see how complaints are being handled now and who is handling them. Ask these individuals what they look for in a customer's complaint. If you find that they look for cases of fraud your company may have unwittingly set the wrong tone. However if you find that they are more concerned with helping the customer, you have a winner.

Option #1

In general, all complaints will be handled as quickly and quietly as possible, so as not to jeopardize the company's good will and reputation.

Much money is expended to secure a customer and generally build up public relations. Handling complaints on a miserly basis can be costly.

Option #2

Merchandise Returned—These decisions must be made by local management. In general we would prefer not to take back gifts, chemicals or equipment that are not faulty but which are returned only because the customer changed his mind. Consider: [1] Is the merchandise still saleable? [2] Was it purchased at regular retail price from us? Does the customer have the sales slip? If management decides to accept the return, then insist that other merchandise be taken in trade, rather than giving a cash refund.

Guarantee—Our guarantees are fair and are on display in the store as well as on the back of the sale's slip. We stand behind the guarantee as written. Customers will sometimes try to take advantage of even our liberal guarantee. *Use good judgment.*

Option #3

Due to the cost of acquiring customers, it is a high priory that we maintain their good will for future possible business and to prevent ill will and bad feelings from spreading through the comments of a disgruntled customer. When we have an irate customer talking to anyone who will listen, you can be sure that our competitors will see that the comments are carried far and wide.

Treat all customer complaints as a challenge to see how well you can treat another human. In general, all complaints will be handled as quickly and quietly as possible, so as not to jeopardize the company's good will and reputation. If you feel that extenuating circumstances are involved, contact your supervisor for advice

Option #4

Use good judgment—When dealing with customer complaints, the operative policy is *use good judgment.* We have used a great deal of time, money, and skill to get this customer. Don't lose him by a quick word.

Our guarantees are fair and reasonable, so *use good judgment* when speaking to a customer about a problem. It may be a simple problem that can be solved quickly. *Don't make it into a major problem.*

Anytime a customer complaint seems to be getting out of hand, call your supervisor for assistance.

Customer Credit

The extension of credit to a customer is an area of just concern due to the possibility that the company may not be paid for goods or services for which resources have already expended. Because the failure of many companies have resulted from poor credit policies, you should give studied attention to what policies will best suit the needs of your customers and your company. A too stringent policy could cause loss of business and a too lenient policy will risk too much capital. The weight given each of these factors you settle on should also on whether you have a high-volume, low-profit operation or a low volume, high profit operation.

You should also give attention to selecting the personnel who will be responsible for administering these policies. Should you choose a person with a pleasant phone voice and great compassion, yet little force of personality, then when payroll is due, you may discover that your bank account is empty.

Option #1

Primarily our business is cash and carry. If, however, a customer presses to charge, credit may extended if the credit manager has investigated and approved the credit. Credit forms are furnished and must be turned in advance for approval and use. The credit manager's approval is necessary for each transaction.

Option #2

All employees are responsible for the proper handling of credit and must comply with the guidelines approved by management and administered by the credit manager. Only the credit manager is authorized to extend credit.

Customer Charges

– must have approval of the credit manager

- must be current
- must have an approved credit application on file

Credit Card Charges
- check cards against stop list
- if over $50 clear with bank
- charges may not exceed purchases

Company Charges
- check account status with credit manager
- get purchase order number or verify with customer's purchasing department

Option #3

This company has a stringent policy for the granting of credit. It is the responsibility of all employees to see that these policies are adhered to. Only the credit may modify them.

1. All new charge sales must be approved either by a manager or credit department.
2. A credit file will be established showing accounts which are approved or disapproved for credit and credit limit and current status.
3. All accounts are due on the 10th of the month.
4. Accounts receivable files are closed to all employees except accounting staff.

Option #4

All charges for all work are due upon completion of the work. If there is any reason you can not pay upon completion, notify us before work begins.

Customer Treatment

Business exist because of customers. Everything a company does has an effect on its customers, and how customers view the company is one of the most important aspects of business. It is therefore important for any company to establish a policy of how customers are to be treated. The tone you establish is what your employees will follow.

Option #1

All of us must remember that the customer is our sole reason for being in business. We must continue to give quality service and strive to improve our service.

Therefore, we are always pleased to do what we can to help our employees' improve their technical abilities and to encourage them to better themselves and thereby, the company. Please do not hesitate to come to your supervisor on any problems on any suggestions or questions you may have.

Option #2

The image you project and the image you leave is the customer's image of the company. The reputation of the company has been dutifully earned over many years of hard service. You can enjoy great satisfaction in being part of one of the finest companies in the industry. You are expected to uphold this tradition.

Option #3

Always remember:

- Greet Clients Promptly - Even one minute is a long time when you are waiting.

- Call Your Client by Name - The most important name in the world is his own.
- Smile - A smile is a trademark of a friendly person. It creates confidence.
- Sell Your Company - When you talk well of your company, you talk well of yourself.
- Don't Argue - You may win an argument but lose a customer.
- Show Your Appreciation - A customer does not feel that you are doing him a favor by serving him.
- Be A Good Listener - Most people would rather talk than listen.
- Say "Thank You" - Make it a habit. It will make your clients happy.
- Do Small Favors - A little act of courtesy means a great deal to our clients.
- Keep Promises - Mean what you say. Confidence is the foundation of good business and friendship.
- Know Your Job - Customers depend on your advice. If you guess, you may guess wrong.
- Look The Part - People judge others by their appearance.
- Keep Cool - Lost tempers lose clients.
- Above All - Demonstrate a willingness, ability, and desire to get the job done right *the first time.*

Option #4

Each employee, no matter what his task, should realize that he is a representative of the company and shall treat each customer as if that customer were the only customer, knowing if it were not for customers there would be no salaries paid.

Delivery/Freight Policy

When establishing a delivery or freight policy remember that delivery and/or freight service will be considered a normal service and must be offered to all customers or it might be construed as an infraction of certain fair trade laws (i.e., restraint of trade as one customer may have an economic advantage over another if you show favoritism).

You may retain flexibility by using generalized statements and specific or special offers from time to time as a sales incentive.

Guidelines to operate with help your employees, so you might wish to address delivery and freight if only to assist them in being more efficient

Option #1

Generally we are not staffed for regular deliveries. However, decisions will be made on a case-by-case basis based on work load and availability of vehicles. If you feel a valuable customer has an unusual need, bring it to the attention of your supervisor.

Option #2

Freight is prepaid on orders over $2,000. All other orders will be sent freight collect. Charges will be prepaid and added to your bill unless you request freight collect. If you do not have an established account and need fast service, we will ship COD.

Option #3

Shipments over $1,000 within the city will be shipped on company vehicles at no charge. If out of the city freight will be paid by the customer. Shipments of less than $999.99 will have a $25.00 delivery charge added if in the city and will be shipped freight collect if out of the city.

Option #4

In order to be as competitive as possible, we bill our customers only for the services they use. If you have the ability to pick up, then you will not be charged for freight shipping. If we can speed your needs along by shipping, we will prepay and add freight to your shipment.

Customer Discounts

In today's economy it has become an accepted practice to allow for commercial discounts. Normal discount policies are aimed at retail companies doing business in the commercial sector, as commercial companies prices tend to have already placed themselves competitively. Your own price structure will be chipped away more by your employee's attitudes of value rather than by the customer concern for cost. Your employees' values of fairness and ethnics should be considered carefully as you make a discount policy and your own actions will be judged against your stated discount policy, so make sure you can live with the policy you establish.

When establishing a discount policy, remember that this will come to be considered a normal price and must be offered to all customers or it may be construed as an infraction of certain fair trade laws (i.e., restraint of trade, as one customer may have an economic advantage over another by your show of favoritism). It is quite acceptable to meet a competitor's price, but you should be careful if you decide to do more than that.

Option #1

Janitorial maintenance companies, hotels, and other such commercial accounts will be sold at the national commercial price list.

Dealers will be sold at the national dealer price list.

Churches and allied nonprofit institutions will be allowed a courtesy discount of 15%.

Option #2

Our pricing structure is based on size of orders. Deviations from our normal pricing are allowed only if a member of management authorizes it. See you supervisor first.

Option #3

We are an aggressive company which is a result of our employees' care and concern for this company. We want you help maintain our competitiveness. Our greatest source of market information is *you*. If competitors find new methods of attracting our customers' only our employees can kept the company informed. Our prices are very fair and competitive but there may be ways that our competitors may use, to try to obtain our customers business. Our regular price list is fair, but if your customer is receiving prices or other services that we are not yet offering, immediately bring the matter to the attention of your supervisor. Only he can authorize changes in prices.

Option #4

As a competitive inducement to acquire commercial business, we allow a 20% discount to all commercial accounts if requested.

CHAPTER 7

OTHER CONSIDERATIONS

Ethical Statement

Although not a necessity, a statement concerning the ethical standards your company adheres to is often a component in the policy manual of an organization meant to weather the test of time. Including a statement of the ethics often strengthens and invigorates the organization by raising the awareness of its personnel through their exposure to and acceptance of those standards and other social responsibilities.

Your needs may not require a completely separate document, but it is worth your considering whether a statement of ethical content is in the best interest of your company. Inclusion of an ethics statement is unlikely to cause damage; and for fields such as banking, it may be essential as one of the principle foundations of the firm. Relying as they do on the public's perception of their solid nature, such companies are well advised to have a separate document concerning the ethical standards that they must project to the public. It is quite possible that such a firm would include strong wording as to the consequences of stepping outside the boundaries of this statement.

Whatever you decide are your needs, make sure that your statement is tempered with courtesy to your employees and their good sense.

Expense Reimbursement

Occasionally it is most efficient for an employee to use personal funds for company purposes whether it may be postage due or major repairs in an out-of-the-way area. You should establish guidelines now so as not to be caught unprepared later. It is also a good idea to state a limit of time when expense reports must be turned in for processing. (One of my ex-employees turned in $1,900 of vague expenses the his last day of employment.)

Option #1

All expenses incurred for company purposes will be turned in for approval and processing as soon as possible, but not after 30 days, and returned in your next pay cycle.

Option #2

Expense Reports will be turned in on the 1st and 15th of each month, and approved expenses will be processed for inclusion within the next pay period.

Option #3

All expenses over $50 must be approved by your supervisor before being incurred and then turned in within seven days for reimbursement.

Option #4

Any expenses not covered under normal circumstances must receive approval of your supervisor and be turned in immediately.

Garnishment of Wages

In some states the only garnishments allowed are those from the federal government, yet the way you approach how your company will view a garnishment is a statement of you, your firm, and the caliber of employees that make your firm what it is.

Option #1

The company views the garnisheeing of earnings as an unnecessary nuisance resulting from poor management of personal finances. Repeated garnishments may be taken into consideration in evaluating an employee's performance.

Option #2

The company is a respected member of the community, and our reputation depends largely upon our employees. Although we understand that a wage garnishment can happen to anyone, we strongly discourage repetition of the original mistake. If an employee repeatedly incurs wage garnishments, his employment may be terminated.

Option #3

All employees are expected to pay their just debts. If any garnishments are levied upon any employee, a moderate weekly payment plan agreeable to all parties will be worked out in writing and signed by all parties. A copy will be filed in the employee's personnel file record. Any employee who accumulates a total of four or more garnishments shall be subject to immediate termination of employment.

It must be understood that if the company works out a payment plan of garnishment, that the company will deduct from the employee employee's wages an additional 10% of the amount withheld to cover costs and bookkeeping.

Gifts and Gratuities

Although most companies and their employees have an understanding of what is proper for acceptance from a client or supplier, it would behoove you to state an official policy. The enactment of a policy relieves your employees of not wishing to seem less than cordial by giving them the excuse of saying that company policy does not allow them to accept this gift.

In my part of the world it is normal for business acquaintances to be treated to an outdoor event such as hunting or fishing, yet it would be highly questionable for the host to present a supplier with a $5,000 boat or $2,000 custom shotgun.

Option #1

Our company has placed trust in our employees by hiring and the placing them in positions of responsibility. We understand that business relationships can develop into personal relationships, but we do not allow some forms of gratitude to be expressed by lavish gifts. All gifts from whatever supplier or client must be declared to management.

Option #2

It is our policy that gifts of any nature be discouraged from suppliers and clients. If you can not discourage a gift, then we do make allowance and have arranged for the American Red Cross to receive it.

Option #3

We do not allow any supplier to gift any employee.

Option #4

As we have placed trust in you by the position you hold, we also place trust in your judgment as regards accepting gifts.

Parking

Parking does not necessarily have to become a policy, but you might want to consider making it so, especially if you have congested parking problems or if you need to keep the areas immediately adjacent to your store entrance open for customer use.

Option #1

Parking space is made available for employees. Unless assigned a specific space, employees should park in (general lot location). Those employees brought to work by someone else are requested to have the driver drop them off and pick them up in the employee parking lot to avoid traffic congestion.

Option #2

The company has established special employment parking areas, and all employees will park their cars in that location.

Option #3

The company has established special employee parking in the north parking lot. All employees will park their cars in this lot. There will be no exceptions.

Option #4

Monday through Friday employees will park cars in areas aligned with the north side of the customer parking lot. On Saturdays, Sundays, and holidays, employees will park their cars in the area located adjacent to the equipment parking lot. There are no exceptions.

Personal Appearance

One of the primary judgments made about your company is based upon the appearance of your personnel. You have every right to expect any employee to conform to some set standard of appearance. Some companies have made the "uniform" of their industry exactly what the standard requirements of their employees wear.

Curious? What computer company first required dark suits with white shirts. What dress code do most high tech companies now demand of their sales staff.

Option #1

All employees are expected to appear in a manner that will reflect favorably upon themselves and upon the company. This includes coming to work well groomed and neatly attired.

All full-time employees are required to wear the company uniform at all times when working for the company. Uniforms are to be worn for work only and not to be worn in public for shopping, etc.

Option #2

We are in the business of serving a discerning class of customers. Everyone will be expected to represent the company in a manner befitting our organization's image in the community. Whether one is a salesman, delivery man, manager, or director, each person is expected to be discreet in his conduct and conservative in grooming and dress.

MEN:

Men are expected to wear company uniforms when provided. Uniforms are to be laundered as needed. Report worn or damaged uniforms to your manager for replacement. The uniform shirts may be worn with the top button left open.

Beards are permitted if closely trimmed. Neatly trimmed mustaches not extending beyond the corners of the mouth or below the upper lip are permitted. Men will otherwise be clean-shaven. Sideburns will not extend below earlobes nor will hair extend below the collar tops or cover any portion of the ear. Hair will be kept neatly combed to the head.

WOMEN:

Ladies are expected to wear company uniforms when provided. Uniforms are to be laundered as needed. Report worn or damaged uniforms to your manager for replacement. When uniforms are not provided, ladies may wear conservatively-styled dresses or pant suits in coordinated colors. Extremes in styles or length in skirts will not be permitted. Since styles are a matter of taste ladies are advised to groom themselves according to the mode of other company employees and are advised not to lean toward extremes.

Hair style will be neat and conservative. Jewelry may be worn so long if discreet. Ladies may wear high heeled or flat shoes. Sandals, boots, open shoes, or tennis shoes are not permitted.

Option #3

Since grooming and dress are personal matters, management sets only general guidelines for employees to follow. However, management will judge each person individually and will direct the employee's attention to those areas which are deemed to need attention and correction.

Phone Use

An often abused privilege is the personal use of company telephones on company time, thereby tying up valuable phone lines and stopping productivity of the employee who abuses the privilege. What is worse is that the abuse seems to spread almost as if a disease were spreading uncontrollably.

When deciding the posture your firm will assume, it might be worth considering how your employees will view the policy you make. Although I rarely recommend a strong posture on any subject because firm postures tend to limit flexibility, in this instance normally you can easily show employees the need for a restricted use of company time and company telephones.

Option #1

Our telephones are heavily loaded with business calls during working hours. These calls have priority, of course, so we must ask you to make personal calls only when necessary and during your lunch period or after working hours. Please discourage others from calling you during working hours.

Option #2

The telephone is a vital and necessary part of our business. With the exception of emergencies, do not use company phones for personal calls. Request your friends to call you at home instead of at work.

The company is not in a position to handle personal mail. Employees should request their personal mail be addressed to their home.

Option #3

Incoming and outgoing personal telephone calls are discouraged during working hours unless they are of an emergency nature.

Option #4

In order to keep company telephone lines open for necessary business calls, employees are requested to discourage any but emergency incoming personal calls. Outgoing personal calls, except in an emergency, are to be made outside of working hours. Only emergency calls will be delivered to employees. Other incoming calls will be posted on the bulletin board.

Option #5

Company phones are not for personal use. Outgoing personal calls should be made on the pay phones provided for this purpose. Incoming personal calls cannot be passed through the switchboard. In the event of an incoming call regards an emergency, the call will be passed to an employee's supervisor who will relay the message.

Option #6

Incoming and outgoing personal telephone calls are discouraged during working hours except in the event of emergencies.

Religious and Political Activities

Religious or political activities can occasionally establish barriers between customers and the company. They can also foster differences that detract from the efficiency of the work force. Furthermore, benefits to the company are not readily apparent. It may therefore be in the best interest of the company to restrict such activities or ban them altogether during company time and on company premises.

Although you may not direct any employee's activities on his own time, you do have the right to decide what is correct for your company and you have the right to expect that policy to be complied with.

Option #1

No activity concerning religious or political advocation is permitted on company time or on company premises.

Option #2

Religious and political activities are not permitted on company time or on company premises unless prior authorization is given in writing by an officer of this organization.

Option #3

This company is proud of the freedoms and opportunities that we are allowed to operate in and believes that the same freedoms should be allowed to our employees. If you have a desire to speak or to provide information to other employees, contact your supervisor for details.

Option #4

To allow the company to operate at its highest efficiency and be viewed by the public as a professional company, all employees are asked to use judgment in the demonstration of religious or political beliefs.

Religious/Ethnic Events

Employees of certain religious and ethnic backgrounds are directed by their beliefs to participate or observe special courses of action during the year. You should give some consideration as to what these needs are and what action you will allow. This advance preparation can will almost certainly be appreciated by those specific members of your work force and build loyalty that cannot be bought.

Option #1

We encourage our employees to support the company with your punctuality and attendance; however, we also understand that occasions of religious or ethnic responsibility require you to meet those demands, too. We need to know in advance what special needs and considerations you have. Report these needs to your supervisor at least two weeks in advance so he may make any needed adjustments for the continuation of production.

Option #2

At the discretion of the company, work loads permitting, employees will be allowed to absent themselves for the observation of special religious or ethnic observances.

Option #3

If you have a special religious or ethnic need to be absent from work, consult with your supervisor for permission.

Safety Regulations

Many safety and health regulations are dictated by federal laws and insurance requirements. Employee compliance is more easily obtained if the employee understands why these policies are in place. It is strongly recommended that you make an effort to explain why their support in complying with these rules is needed.

Most employees will try to be more efficient (by bypassing safety standards) than you can afford, especially from the cost of workman's compensation and increased insurance. Your company's attitude will be the most important factor for compliance an employee will honor. It is to your benefit to make sure employees see a strong need to help you in complying with safety standards.

Option #1

The company will strive to provide a clean, safe, and healthy place to work. Employees are expected to do their part, to work safely, wear required safety equipment, observe all posted safety rules and regulations, and keep their work area neat and clean.

Personal safety equipment such as gloves, glasses, and hard-soled shoes will be provided by each employee at his own expense when they are required. Other safety devices, such as hard helmets and respirators, will be provided by the company when their use is dictated. Any accident, no matter how slight, is to be reported at once.

Option #2

The company feels that a clean, safe, and healthy environment is the right of all employees. Employees are expected to do their part—to work safely, wear required safety equipment, observe all safety rules and regulations, and keep their work area neat and clean. The company complies with all the regulations of the Occupational Safety and Health Act (OSHA) and requests that employees report any unsafe situation to their supervisors so it can be corrected.

Option #3

Employees are to report all injuries sustained on the job at once. Supervisors will have first aid equipment and will arrange for medical or hospitalization if needed.

Option #4

A Safety Committee considers all safety recommendations made by employees. An award of $10 will be paid to the employee submitting the most worthwhile safety suggestion each month. Also, an award is made at the end of the year for the safety suggestion considered by the Committee to be the most worthy.

Option #5

The company wants to provide you with a safe work area with the least possible risk of injury. Although we have an established safety program, we need your cooperation to make it work well. If you observe all of the safety requirements for the job, you'll be protecting not only yourself but your co-workers as well. If there is anything you consider to be unsafe in your area, please report it immediately to your area safety captain whose name is posted on the bulletin board.

Option #6

Accidents don't just happen—they are caused. Your safety is a matter of major concern to the company. Every reasonable caution is taken to provide you with a safe place to work. However, without the sincere and faithful cooperation of all employees, safety programs alone are of little value in preventing accidents. Accident prevention is largely the responsibility of each individual.

Option #7

The company will strive to provide a clean, safe, and healthy place to work. Employees are expected to do their part, to work safely, wear required safety equipment, observe all posted safety rules and regulations, and keep their place neat and clean.

Personal safety equipment such as gloves, glasses, hard sole shoes, will be provided by each employee at his own expense. Any accident, no matter how slight, is to be reported to your supervisor at once.

Industrial illness and accidents are covered by Workman's Compensation Insurance.

Security Policy

Security of physical items such as documents, files, equipment, inventory, and money should not be assumed but mandated by a firm policy. It has come to the attention of some organizations that if you do not prepare an understandable and workable policy about security, then items of major importance tend to disappear. You may be able to get the cooperation of all employees by engaging in a roundtable discussion with those personnel who are directly involved with the handling of company assets. In fact you may be surprised by the multitude of innovative ways they are aware of about how company assets can disappear. Listen to them: they are the people who know.

Option #1

All employees who have been authorized to handle the assets of the company are charged with seeing that such items are protected to the best extent practicable. If you see a way that helps in this responsibility, immediately bring the matter to the attention of your supervisor.

Option #2

Any employee who is entrusted with the assets of the company is charged with protecting those assets to the best of his abilities. You are not, however, to offer physical resistance to a robbery or theft, but to do exactly as requested. However, you are charged will reporting any potential for loss to your supervisor for action.

Smoking

The fear of not attracting or not retaining the best employees has caused some employers to skirt this issue. It might be interesting to consider whether a person would be a better employee for your company if he chose to demonstrate of his own self-worth by not using tobacco.

A smoking policy is discretionary if you employ fewer than 20 employees. Smoking is covered by the EEOC regulations for offices if you employ more than 20 people. OSHA regulations apply around hazardous or flammable materials. Most states have addressed smoking, and many cities have established ordnances concerning smoking in public places, especially where food is served. You should check with local regulators for applicable information before establishing your smoking policy.

Certain manufacturing processes, such as delicate electronic assembly, and sterile sanitary fields, such as hospital operating rooms, dictate "No Smoking" by the nature of their sensitivity to airborne particulate.

In several instances total bans have been placed upon smoking as a condition of employment. One of the most widely published is the case of a governmental body who made it a policy that employees were not allowed to smoke any time due to increased health care costs after retirement.

You do have the right to make your working environments "No Smoking" areas. Or, you may utilize other methods to limit discomfort to nonsmokers. Your best sources of information are your employees. Ask them in a quiet, discrete way what they want. More and more companies are adopting "No Smoking" or "No Smoker" policies as a way to improve employee health, save money, increase productivity, lower absenteeism, and protect themselves against expensive litigation.

If you adopt a "No Smoking" or "No Smoker" policy, you should address your insurance costs, as some insurance companies will lower rates for auto, liability, and medical policies based upon smoking bans.

Current behavioral research indicates that smoking is both an addiction and a habit, which may suggest the need for support programs or assistance in quitting, in the event of establishing a total ban on smokers. Several nonprofit groups such as the American Lung Association can offer assistance through "Stop Smoking Clinics" and educational material. If you choose to have a total ban upon hiring smokers, then you might wish to title this section "Nonsmoking Policy," thereby making it the norm.

Option #1

Smoking is permitted only in areas designated as smoking areas. (Some city ordnances require this.)

Option #2

Smoking is not permitted in company offices or buildings. (This can be expanded to include company vehicles, as well.)

Option #3

Smoking is a personal matter and is an individual decision to be made by our employees. However, you are required to be observant of the needs and feelings of nonsmoking people around you. Your courtesy can prevent the establishment of a hard-line "No Smoking" policy or a dedicated smoking areas program.

Option #4

It is the policy of this firm not to employ any person who uses tobacco products. If you are a tobacco user, it is understood as a condition of employment that you will quit the use of tobacco during your probationary period and not resume tobacco use at any time during your employment. The use of tobacco in any form is prohibited during "on" company time and "off" company time.

Social Events

Social employee events are often recommended as a method for allowing positive interaction among employees. People in a relaxed atmosphere with enjoyable activities are more prone to bond together, and a cohesive group tends to accomplish more in the work environment.

In addition to the positive effects of having social events, however, you should also consider the possible risks and liability exposure if accidents occur or, in light of the new wave of extended exposure, if alcohol is provided.

Option #1

From time to time, the company sponsors events which create an opportunity for all families in the company to gather and become better acquainted. Getting to know one another better helps create a better place in which to work.

Option #2

We are supportive of various social and civic recreational activities for our employees. Special events are scheduled in advance for all employees. You and your family are urged to attend, participate, and have fun with your co-workers. These are fun events. We welcome your suggestions concerning an event or theme.

Option #3

Social events are sponsored by the company for the development of better relations of all employees. Your participation in these activities is actively sought. We can become a better company only with your support and we hope you will help make these events a success.

Solicitations

As you decide what your best course of action should be, do not be deluded into thinking that a secretary selling plastic ware or cosmetics is engaging in an innocent pastime. You are paying not only for her time but also for the time lost to other employees who are subjected to paying attention to her rather than to business. In addition, solicitations by fellow employees may become matter of concern and action to employers due to negative reactions if items sold are not as represented. You might then have to become an arbitrator in a business transaction that does not profit the company.

Option #1

The solicitation of any nature by an employee is requires the approval of management.

Option #2

Before an employee may sell or solicit in any way for any item not directly related to the company, a written authorization is required by an officer of the company.

Option #3

Only solicitation for nonprofit causes and then only on free time is allowed by employees.

Tools and Supplies

It is in the best interest of your company to know where your assets are. Equipment, tools, and supplies are more than likely one of your largest assets and costs, especially when they are not available when needed or not in inventory as thought to be. The cost of downtime and lost efficiency while one employee or a whole crew stops work either to track down the items or to purchase replacements can be staggering.

You should address some thought as to how your company should view this topic. Do employees furnish their own tools or does the company? Generally, in smaller companies, hand tools and the like can be furnished by the company as a way of insuring good equipment for highest productivity. In larger companies, however, theft and misplacement may provide reason for the employee either to check tools out and be responsible for their cost or to own them himself depending on circumstances.

In most situations, larger pieces of equipment are assets of the company and thereby covered by the company's liability insurance. Keep in mind, however, that the tools your company uses are for your company's use. Unless you have specific insurance coverage for their use outside of company supervision, you should use care in how you approach the lending of tools. Although it is improbable that the words written on your typewriter would be cause for a damage suit to your company, it is conceivable that a fire resulting from a defective appliance would. If you opt to allow unsupervised use of company equipment, consult both your legal consul and your insurance liability carrier.

Option #1

Employees are asked to put up a deposit on personal hand tools (i.e., pliers, cutters, and so forth). The deposit will be in the amount of the cost of the item. Should you wear out the tool, a new one will be exchanged at no additional cost; however, the tool must have been properly used. Should you leave employment, the deposit will be returned to you after you turn in your tools.

Some tools will be provided without deposit, but it is your responsibility to maintain and put away these tools.

Transfer of materials, whether within the company, between departments, or outside the company, will occur only with the proper written authorization.

Option #2

All trucks, tractors, trailers, and miscellaneous tools, equipment, and supplies are the property of the company, either by direct ownership or lease thereof. These tools are provided for you to perform the work you are assigned and are issued to the foreman in charge and are his responsibility. These tools, if lost or mishandled through neglect, will be charged against the foreman and will be deducted from his wage at the year's end. Any additional tools or equipment checked out from the tool crib for special use or purpose will also be charged to the foreman. They must be returned or replaced after work is completed.

From time to time, it will be necessary to put various equipment to use for general projects. At that time, some other person will be assigned for operation. Responsibility for any damage, mechanical or otherwise, to the equipment during the period of temporary assignment will be handled as follows:

Both the permanently assigned employee and temporarily assigned employee will check the equipment prior to use and note any discrepancy. Upon return to the permanent assignee, both parties will again check and report any discrepancies.

It is not a policy of this company to provide equipment or tools for any personal use at any time. No licensed equipment will remain away from company premises overnight.

Option #3

Some company-owned tools or equipment may be loaned to employees. If you would like to use a tool, make an application to the manger at least one week prior to the desired use for approval. In such cases, all responsibilities for damages, gas, oil, and liability remain with the employee. Equipment must be inspected with the supervisor upon returning to the company use. No licensed equipment will remain away from company premises overnight.

Option #4

All trucks, tractors, trailers, miscellaneous tools, equipment, and supplies are the property of the company, either by direct ownership or lease. These tools are provided for employees to perform the work they are assigned and are issued to the foreman in charge and are his responsibility.

Option #5

Supervisors will tell employees the kind and number of tools the company requires them to furnish. Many tools will be issued by the Tool Room. Supervisors will explain how to draw out and return them. Tools are to be returned when there is no immediate need for them. If an employee loses a tool or fails to check it in for any reason, the cost of this tool will be deducted from his paycheck. Employees will not be charged for tools which are broken when being properly used.

Option #6

Some company-owned tools or equipment may be borrowed by employees for their brief personal use. Employees wishing this privilege should make an application to the manager at least one week prior to the desired use. In such cases, all responsibility for damages, gas, oil, and liability remain with the employee. Equipment must be inspected with the supervisor present, upon being returned for company use. No licensed equipment will remain away from company premises overnight.

Additions:
The company does not lend tools, vehicles, or other equipment to employees under any circumstances.

Uniforms

Depending on the nature of your business, you may want to weigh the merits of uniforms for your company. Most fast food restaurant chains supply uniforms; so do most motor freight companies. They feel that identifying their employees to customers allows for faster service and greater efficiency. The fast food customer immediately knows who can take his order. The motor freight employee does not waste time verbally verifying his business but is hurried along his way since the customer wants speedy freight service.

Uniforms need be neither custom designed nor fitted; the largest chain of convenience stores uses smocks to identify clerks on duty. Your company may decide that printed T-shirts fulfill your needs. A side benefit is that all your employees become walking billboards keeping your company's name in front of the public.

Option #1

As an employee of the company, after one year of continuous service, you will be issued three clean uniforms and will be expected to be neatly dressed in them when on duty. The company will pay for one-half the cost of cleaning. The balance is a payroll deduction. Uniforms are picked up for cleaning at the Office twice a week on Tuesdays and Fridays. You will be expected to turn in soiled uniforms on these days; otherwise, you will be required to clean your own uniforms. If you should leave employment with the company for any reason, the uniform is to be returned or the value thereof will be deducted from your last pay.

It is a company directive that all employees working in the field will provide themselves with and wear heavy work shoes at all times.

The company asks that you do not wear your uniform on off-duty periods. We do not feel that it is good advertisement to be seen with a uniform in a night club, etc., in the evening. This uniform is work clothing only, not a supplement to your regular clothes. New employees are directed to wear white T-shirts and blue trousers to work until eligible for uniform issue. You are expected to be well groomed and neat on the job at all times. Excessively long hair is not permitted. No short pants or irregular clothing will be permitted on the job.

Remember, your appearance creates the public image of the company!

Option #2

The company supplies seven sets of uniforms to all employees. This allotment provides for three sets at your home, three sets in the wash, and one being worn, allows for two days' wear of each uniform. Employees wanting a clean uniform for every day can increase the allotment to 11 sets by paying a charge for additional uniforms. All employees are eligible to rent uniforms at their own expense after having worked four weeks with the company.

Option #3

Work uniforms will be provided by the company for all retail sales personnel. You will receive five sets if full-time employed. You will only wear one uniform for two work days. Uniforms for men include work jackets. Women will be provided with initialed smocks to be worn over suitable work outfits. Laundry and cleaning will be at employee's expense.

The uniforms, jackets, and smocks are paid for by and are the property of the company. Upon termination, employees must return the uniforms.

Vehicle Policy

A company with a good vehicle policy is in a much better position to handle emergency situations. You would be well advised to give careful attention to the selection of issues you want addressed by your vehicle policy. Most companies make statements concerning driving safety, cleanliness, accidents, maintenance, alcohol, personal use, and drugs-both illegal and prescription.

Option #1

Company vehicles may be operated on public roads only by specifically authorized employees who possess all licenses required by local law. All accidents must be reported to the office immediately.

Option #2

CONDITION—Company vehicles are expect to be neat and clean inside and out at all times. Any defective operation in any vehicle should be noted to the supervisor each day in writing on the form provided. The first day of every month, crew leader in charge of specific power equipment will make out the performance reports.

ACCIDENTS—All accidents will be reported to the office immediately. An accident involving a company vehicle which is determined to be the fault of a company employee through carelessness or neglect will be charged against that employee.

Option #3

CONDITION—Company vehicles are expected to be neat and clean inside and out as far as possible at all times. Any defective operation of any vehicle should be noted to the mechanic each day in writing on the form provided. The first day of every month the foreman in charge of specific power equipment will make out performance reports.

ACCIDENTS—Company vehicles are insured for liability only. All accidents will be reported to the office immediately. An accident involving a company vehicle which is determined to be the fault of a company employee through carelessness or neglect may be charged against that employee.

GAS AND OIL—The company purchases gas and oil lubricants. These supplies are for use in company vehicles only. All gas and oil will be recorded by the mechanic and monthly checks made. Use of gas in personal cars is forbidden.

Option #4

Company vehicles are assigned to the management and are for the general use and promotion of business. Company vehicles are not for personal use.

Option #5

The company does not lend vehicles or other equipment to employees under any circumstances.

Weather Policy

At some point you will probably begin to wonder how many topics to include in a policy manual, and a weather policy may appear dispensable. Yet, in some areas of the country weather is an important aspect of business, especially for those involved in outdoor work. Consider sunny Florida where almost every business is open all year round, but every once in awhile they have severe storms.

Option #1

You are to report for work, regardless of weather conditions. When at all possible, work will be assigned; when not, you will be dismissed as quickly as possible and one hour of pay credited for reporting when sent home due to weather. Daily inclement weather lay-off shall follow the seniority. An employee will be entitled to reporting pay unless he was told not to report for work. Such notice is not required to employees who were absent when others were told not to report.

Option #2

Since no outdoor work can be done during periods of bad weather, hourly employees who work outdoors should not report to work when it is raining hard. If you have any question as to whether there will be work on a given day, telephone your supervisor. Salaried employees will not be paid if they do not call in.

Option #3

Unless otherwise instructed, employees are to report for work, regardless of weather conditions. When at all possible, work will be assigned; when not, employees will be dismissed as quickly as possible and one hour of pay credited for reporting when sent home due to weather. Daily inclement weather layoff shall follow seniority. An employees will be entitled to reporting pay unless he was told not to report to work. Such notice is not required to employees who were absent when others were told not to work.

Option #4

Unless otherwise instructed, employees are to report for work, regardless of weather conditions. Employees are guaranteed half pay in the morning on bad days for a minimum of two hours. Employees must be present at 7:00 a.m. to qualify.

Option #5

All full-time, seasonal, and part-time employees who work outdoors will be paid one hour at their regular rate if they report to work and are unable to work because of bad weather conditions. To be eligible for show-up time, an employee must report to work on time, remain on the premises until the supervisor gives a release and signs the timecard for the day in question. An employee must accept other work on that day if offered or else forfeit the show-up time.

APPENDIX A

SAMPLE OF WELCOME LETTERS

Dear New Employee,

We at the ABC Company want to welcome you to our company. We have strived to make this one of the finest companies of its kind in the world and we ask your support in continuing with that goal. Your suggestions and positive comments are sought at all times. We even go to extra lengths to make you aware of our appreciation by giving special cash incentives and awards for productive observations.

Our firm is very involved with trust yours, ours, and the public's, so you will easily understand the burning desire of management and all of our employees to strive for excellence in maintaining the image we have struggled so long to acquire. Our trust in your experience and judgment is evidenced by our decision to employ you. We ask that at any point where you see either us or the company not living up to our potential to let us know immediately.

You should have been provided with a copy of our company policy manual for a more detailed statement of our philosophy, goals, objectives and topics that will bear upon all aspects of our association. Although many companies have not taken the time and effort to provide their employees with a road map of the company's destination, we have. You see, we screen our personnel very carefully, we want only the best on our team and because of our reputation we are picky, because of our high standards we know that you are self-motivated and can utilize this policy manual to further all our goals.

The purpose of any policy manual is to state the company's objectives and our way of accomplishing those objectives. It is intended to make sure all employees have the same opportunities and benefits and further that we all operate within a standard set of guidelines. It is our objective that these policies are fair and equitable to both the employee and company alike.

Allow all of us at ABC want to take this opportunity to welcome you to a great company.

APPENDIX B

SAMPLE OF POLICY MANUAL EXAMPLE

We at ABC Company have prepared this General Policy Manual so that our employees will have a steady reference guide that will answer questions concerning day to day activities and explain how we want various aspects of the company's affairs handled.

As this is a general guide and not intended to cover every aspect of all activities, then for those specific areas where you need additional direction contact your immediate supervisor.

TABLE OF CONTENTS

22. Parking
23. Personal Appearance
24. Conduct
25. Company Tools and Supplies
26. Company Meetings
27. Use of Company Phone
28. Security Procedures
29. Customer Treatment
30. Complaints
31. Religious and Political Activities
32. Confidential Information
33. Employee Information Disclosure
34. Smoking
35. Harassment/Sexual/Mental
36. Gifts/Gratuities

Employment Policy

It is the policy of the company to make no discrimination because of sex, color, race, age (between ages 45-70), national origin, or religion in its hiring, promotion, and other employment practices. A new employee will be considered a probationary employee for six (6) months after coming on the payroll. At the end of this period, based upon his demonstrated qualities, a decision will be made as to whether or not an individual will become a permanent employee of the company.

Working Hours

The basic work day is eight hours and the basic work-week is 40 hours. Your own hours of work will depend on the needs of the department to which you are assigned. Instructions regarding scheduled days of work and starting and quitting times will be explained by your supervisor.

Pay Periods

The pay period begins on Thursday of each week and ends on Wednesday. Pay day is on a weekly basis which is on Friday. Checks are available at the completion of your workday, covering time worked in the preceding Thursday through Wednesday period.

Expense Reimbursement

All expenses incurred for company purposes will be turned in for approval and processing as soon as possible, but not after 30 days, and returned in your next pay cycle.

Wage and Salary Reviews/Promotions

Present employees will be considered for promotion before new employees are hired for the vacancy. Employees with the required knowledge, skill, ability, interest, and physical fitness will be given a trial test when practical. Length of service will be a factor in determining promotions. Any vacancies will be a factor in determining promotions. Any vacancies likely to last more than 30 days which are not due to temporary causes and which the company decides should be filled, will be filled by promotion of present employees, if reasonably qualified. The company will select the employees to be transferred or promoted to a vacancy from among those who have requested transfer to the vacancy and who have demonstrated their ability to do the job. The company will hire a new employee to fill a vacancy in which no employee has requested promotion.

Attendance

Punctual and consistent attendance is an important factor in determining an employee's continuation and advancement in the company.

If an emergency requires an employee to leave the premises during working hours, the supervisor must first be notified. When an employee knows in advance that they must be absent from work, the supervisor should be notified before that time.

- Employees should write down their supervisor's home phone number so that he may be called if necessary.
- Time lost by salaried employees as a result of repeated tardiness may be deducted from an employee's salary.

Holidays

There are six paid holidays each year. They are: New Year's Day, Memorial Day, July 4th, Labor Day, Thanksgiving and Christmas.

To be eligible for holiday pay, you must be a regular full-time employee. A regular full-time employee is one who has been in the company's employ full-time for three or more months.

Vacations

After one year of continuous employment, you will be entitled to one week of vacation on the anniversary of your hiring date. After two years of employment, you are entitled to two weeks of vacation each year. After ten years of continuous service, you will be entitled to three weeks of vacation each year. All vacations must be taken by December 31 of the calendar year in which the anniversary of your hiring date falls.

Leave of Absence

An unpaid leave of absence for cause may be granted by the company providing it does not seriously disrupt operations. A request for leave will be presented to the Supervisor and Personnel Department. Such leave will be discussed and determined on an individual basis.

Sick and Disability Leave

All full-time employees (40 hours or more per week—hourly or salaried) will accrue sick leave at the following rates:

One-half day leave for each full month of continued employment, with a maximum of six days credit in any one year.

All sick leave pay is computed at eight hours per day straight time. Sick leave pay is not cumulative and cannot be carried over to the following year.

Funeral Leave

Regular, full-time employees are allowed up to three days of paid funeral leave to arrange for and attend the funeral of a member of your immediate family.

Jury Leave

Employees are encouraged to respond to civic duty when called to serve as a member of a jury panel. Regular full-time employees will receive current daily pay, less any payments received for serving from the city or county. To receive Jury Duty leave payment, employees should submit the jury summons along with all records of payments received.

Military Leave

All regular, full-time employees will be granted a leave of absence if called for active duty by a branch of the U.S. Armed Services. Every effort will be made to hold open the vacated position at the current rate of pay.

Moonlighting

Moonlighting is the practice of working a second job for another employer in addition to working for the Company. You may not engage in the sales of goods or services offered by this company in any of its division as a representative of another firm or yourself. This is not consistent with the company's need to have you represent the Company all of the time, both on and off the job. Moonlighting may be permitted if there is no conflict of interest and it does not affect your work performance here. See your supervisor for approval.

Supervisor/Foreman

The supervisor is the person with whom employees will be in daily contact. He will evaluate employees periodically in terms of attendance, attitude, performance, and ability. His recommendations will be one of the most important factors in any merit pay increases. Should an employee have any questions or problems about company policy, or any other matter, he should talk with his supervisor. The supervisor reflects the thoughts of company management, and has complete responsibility.

Termination of Employment/Recall

If an employee has been on the payroll one year, but less than two years, one week's advance notice of termination will be given. The company may, at its discretion, apply one week's wage in lieu of notice. If an employee has been on the payroll two years or more, the company will give either two weeks' notice or pay two weeks wage in lieu of notice. No notice need be given to probationary employees. No advance notice of termination or termination pay need be given if an employee is dismissed because of misconduct, insubordination, or failure to follow company rules.

Regular work will be provided as far as practical. However, because of the seasonal nature of our business, there are times when layoffs are necessary. If a layoff should become necessary, employees will be laid off on the basis of their ability, attendance, length of service, and production records.

All departments will try to schedule work so that employees who must be laid off can be given adequate advance notice. However, it is recognized that there are times when economic conditions make it impossible to give such advance notice. Every effort will be made to call laid-off employees back to work as soon as possible. An employee who declines recall to his regular job will be considered to have quit.

Severance Pay

Where lack of work causes the termination of an employee, and providing the employee has had good performance reviews over the last two reviews, the company will provide two weeks severance in lieu of notice.

Insurance Programs

An attractive insurance program has been adopted by the company for the benefit of employees. Full details are provided in a separate document.

Workman's Compensation

This insurance is provided by the company as required by state law. It provides employees with payments for any injury resulting from an accident while working for the company. These payments begin after the seventh day of total disability. The insurance company names certain doctors to whom an employee must go in order to receive payment under this insurance.

During the period of recovery from a temporary injury, employees will receive payments from the insurance company. These payments will continue until the doctor releases the employee to return to work. If the type of injury requires a period of convalescence, the company will grant a 90-day period before the employee is required to return to work. Regardless of the type of injury, it must be reported promptly and properly.

Suggestion Awards

A Suggestion Awards Committee handles the suggestion awards program within the company. The committee meets every month and awards are made for the best employee suggestions submitted during the month (as long as the committee feels suggestions submitted are worthy of an award). The awards are $15, $10, and $5. In addition, annual awards of $100, $50, and $25 are given for the first, second, and third place suggestions during the previous year.

Many improvements have been made in the company's operation as a result of suggestions made by employees. All should keep their minds open and alert for labor saving or safety suggestions. Supervisors will help prepare any suggestions an employee may have.

Parking

Parking space is made available for employees. Unless assigned a specific space, employees should park in (general lot location). Those employees who are brought to work by someone else are requested to have the person bringing them to work drop them off in the employee parking lot and pick them up at the same place, to avoid traffic congestion.

Personal Appearance

All employees are expected to appear in a manner that will reflect favorably upon themselves and upon the company. This includes coming to work well groomed and neatly attired.

All full-time employees are required to wear the company uniform at all times when working for the company. Uniforms are to be worn for work only and not to be worn in public for shopping, etc.

Conduct

All of us prefer to work in a job situation where our fellow employees cooperate and respect each other's rights. The Company is convinced that common sense and common courtesy are a necessary part of every employee's work habits.

Company Tools and Supplies

Some company-owned tools or equipment may be borrowed by employees for their brief personal use. Employees wishing this privilege should make an application to the manager at lease one week prior to the desired use. In such cases, all responsibility for damages, gas, oil, and liability remain with the employee. Equipment must be checked out with the supervisor upon returning to company use. No licensed equipment will remain away from company premises overnight.

Company Meetings

Company meetings for certain employees will be held during normal working hours at times designated by management. The purpose of such meetings is for the dissemination of information, the solution of common problems, and the advancement of knowledge and understanding of the employees of the company. Attendance at such meetings is mandatory unless excused in advance by a supervisor.

Use of Company Phone

Our telephones are heavily loaded with business calls during working hours. These come first, of course, so we must ask you to make personal calls only when necessary during your lunch period or after working hours. Please discourage others from calling you during working hours.

Security Procedures

All employees who have been authorized to handle the assets of the company are charged with seeing that such items are protected to the best extent that is practicable. If you see a way that helps in this responsibility, immediately bring the matter to the attention of your supervisor.

Customer Treatment

All of us must remember that the customer is our sole reason for being in business. We must continue to give quality service and strive to improve our service.

Therefore, we are always pleased to do what we can to help our people improve their technical abilities and to encourage them to better themselves and thereby, the company. Please do not hesitate to come to us on any problems on any suggestions or questions you may have.

Complaints

In general, all complaints will be handled as quickly and quietly as possible, so as not to jeopardize the company's good will and reputation.

Much money is expended to secure a customer and generally build up public relations—handling complaints on a miserly basis can be costly.

Religious and Political Activities

This company is proud of the freedoms and opportunities that we are allowed to operate in and believe that the same freedoms should be allowed to our employees. If you have a desire to speak or provide information to other employees, contact your supervisor for details.

Confidential Information

It is the policy of this company, that any and all information about our business be treated as strictly confidential and further since our clients expect confidentiality, that any work done for them be treated with the same understanding and agreement.

Employee Information Disclosure

We do not allow any disclosure of any information, of any nature, concerning employees, past employees or customers.

Smoking

Smoking is a personal matter and is an individual decision to be made by our employees. However, you are required to be observant of the needs and feelings of non smoking people around you. Your courtesy can prevent the establishment of a hard line "No Smoking" policy or a dedicated smoking areas program.

Harassment/Sexual/Mental

Harassment by any member of this firm to any other person whether another employee or a customer will be grounds for immediate disciplinary action or dismissal. It is a portion of the agreement of employment that all employees

Gifts/Gratuities

It is our policy that gifts of any nature be discouraged from suppliers and clients. If you can not discourage a gift then we do make allowance and have arranged for the American Red Cross to receive it.

APPENDIX C

SAMPLE MEMORANDA

The ABC Company
123 Main Street
Anytown, USA 12345
Employment Memorandum; Terms and Conditions

1. The ABC Company (hereinafter called the Company) proposes to employ (name of person) (hereinafter called the Employee) as (name of position) in consideration of the Employees acceptance of the terms of this proposal and performance of its agreements. The effective date of this agreement will be (date).
2. In consideration thereof, the Employee agrees to represent the Company devoting full time exclusively to promote the best interest of the Company in the selling of its products and maintaining the goodwill of its present and future customers, and that the Employee will not sell for or in any way represent

other firms or persons without the express permission in writing from the Company.

3. The Employee's area of responsibility shall consist of the that area listed on the attached "Exhibit A." The Company may, at its sole discretion, change or modify the area of responsibility by giving written notice to such effect.

4. As remuneration for the Employees services, the Company agrees to pay the Employee in the method as described in "Exhibit B," attached. The Company reserves the right to reduce any amounts due the Employee by any amounts owed the Company upon termination of this agreement.

5. Customer accounts are Company property and are subject to Company credit and terms of payment requirements. Customers are to make their remittance directly to the Company. In the event collection is made by the Employee, it shall immediately be forwarded to the Company. The Employee is to assist in the collection of past due accounts.

6. The Employee will comply with all rules and regulations of the Company in which its decisions shall be final and will furnish promptly such reports as may from time to time be requested, and shall follow such instructions as may be given.

7. The Employee agrees to contract no debts or obligations in the Company name or in any way binding upon the Company without having first received written authority therefor, and that the Employee will not borrow any money from or contract any personal debts with any customer or employee of a customer, and the Employee agrees to hold the Company free and harmless from any breach thereof by any Employee.

8. The Employee agrees not to disclose to anyone, either during or after employment, any confidential information including, but not limited to, trade secrets, business policies, business methods, forms or names or addresses of customers.

9. The Employee agrees, upon termination of this agreement, to return to the Company immediately all inventory, samples, literature, price lists, correspondence, list of customers, sales manuals, stationery, and other matter, merchandise, or equipment sent or furnished by the Company.

10. The failure of the Company at any time to require performance by the Employee of any provisions hereof shall in no way affect the Company's right thereafter to enforce the same; nor shall the waver by the Company of any breach or provisions thereof be taken or held to be a waver of any succeeding breach of any such provisions or as a waiver of the provision itself.

11. It is mutually agreed that this agreement shall be interpreted, construed and enforced in accordance with the laws of the State of (state name).

12. It is mutually agreed that this agreement shall not become effective until accepted by the Employee hereon, and thereafter approved by an authorized Company officer; and that there are no understandings, representations or agreements outside the terms of this agreement, and that it shall not be modified or amended hereafter, except in writing, executed by the Employee, and approved by an authorized Company officer.

13. This agreement is subject to the review at any calender year end or at any time at the discretion of the Company or at any time at the request of the Employee. In any event, this agreement may be terminated by the Company for cause without notice or at any time for reason by either party upon two weeks written notice. In the event the Company terminates this agreement for cause, it shall determine the effective date of termination. In the event the Company otherwise terminates this agreement, the effective date of termination shall be two weeks following the date that notice is given, and the Company may require the Employee to cease active work at

any time during those two weeks. In the event the Employee terminates this agreement, the Company shall determine the effective date of termination, but such termination date shall not be earlier than the date notice is given nor later than two weeks after such notice is given.

ACCEPTED: (EMPLOYEE)________________________________

ACCEPTED: (HIRING AUTHORITY)________________________

APPROVED: (COMPANY OFFICER)_________________________

The ABC Company
123 Main Street
Anytown, USA 12345

Employment Memorandum; Terms and Conditions
Exhibit A - Areas of Responsibility

Employee's Name____

Effective Date of Agreement ________________________________

Listed below are the (geographic areas or functional or job responsibilities) which make up the Employee's (territory or function):

City
or
State
or
United States
or
Finance
or Accounts Receivable etc.

The Employee is to confine his activities and efforts to those areas indicated above unless otherwise authorized by the Company.

ACCEPTED: (EMPLOYEE)________________________________

ACCEPTED: (HIRING AUTHORITY)_________________________

APPROVED: (COMPANY OFFICER)_________________________

The ABC Company
123 Main Street
Anytown, USA 12345

Employment Memorandum; Terms and Conditions
Exhibit B - Terms of Remuneration

Employee's Name____________________________________

Effective Date of Agreement____________________________

The Company agrees to pay the Employee in the method as described below as full remuneration for the Employee's services. Modification of or amendment to the amount or terms of remuneration may be made by the Company without advance notice upon the written acceptance by both the Company and the Employee.

A. Salary - The Employee will receive an salary of $2,400.00 per month. This will be paid in accordance with applicable Company policy.

B. Bonus - The Employee will receive a bonus of $2,400.00 per quarter if assigned goals are met or exceeded. This will be paid in accordance with applicable Company policy.

C. Commissions - Commissions will be credited to the Employee at time of shipment, but shall later be reduced, amended, or deducted in the case of nondelivery, return, or nonpayment. Commissions will be paid to the Employee monthly in accordance with applicable Company policy.

D. Draw - The Employee will receive an advance loan (draw) against commissions of $2,400.00 (if none, state so) per month. This will be paid in accordance with applicable Company policy.

Travel Expense - The Employee will receive a Travel Allowance of $1,000.00 (if none, so state) per month, paid semimonthly in accordance with applicable Company policy.

In the event the Company terminates this agreement for cause, all remuneration shall cease as of the effective date of termination, and the Company shall not be liable for any draw, commissions covering shipments made, or travel allowance, after the effective date of agreement termination. In the event this agreement is otherwise terminated, the Employee's draw and travel allowance (each prorated in accordance with applicable Company policy) will continue only through the last day of active work, and commissions will be credited to the Employee's account (subject to reduction in accordance with above) only on account of shipments made through the last day of active work. In the event the Company otherwise terminates this agreement and requires the Employee to cease active work on a date before the two weeks' notice period ends, the Employee's draw (prorated in accordance with applicable Company policy) will continue for the days not actively worked during the notice period. In the event, however, the Employee gives two weeks' notice of termination of this agreement and even though the Company may determine an earlier effective date, the Employee's draw (prorated in accordance with applicable Company policy) will continue through the end of the two weeks. Regardless of how this agreement is terminated, the Employee will be paid draw (prorated in accordance with applicable Company policy) on account of any vacation days for which the Employee is eligible which have not been taken.

ACCEPTED: (EMPLOYEE)______________________________

ACCEPTED: (HIRING AUTHORITY)______________________

APPROVED: (COMPANY OFFICER) ______________________

Ten Commandments of Good Service

I. A Customer is the most important person in any business.

II. A Customer is not dependent on us—we are dependent on him.

III. A Customer is not an interruption of our work—he is the purpose of it.

IV. A Customer does us a favor when he buys; we are not doing him a favor by selling him.

V. A Customer is a part of our business—not an outsider.

VI. A Customer is not someone to argue or match wits with.

VII. A Customer is a person who brings us his needs—it is our job to fill his needs.

VIII. A Customer is deserving of the most courteous and attentive treatment we can give him.

IX. A Customer is the fellow that makes it all possible to pay your salary. Treat Him Well !!

X. A Customer is the lifeblood of this and every other business.

Rules of Communication

1. Be willing to support our purpose, games, rules, goals and direction unconditionally.
2. Speak supportively of each person, our association and goals.
3. Acknowledge whatever is being communicated as true for the speaker at that moment.
4. Complete your agreements unconditionally.

    a. Make only agreements that you are willing to keep.
    b. Communicate any potential broken agreements at the first appropriate time.
    c. Clear up any broken agreements at the first appropriate time.

5. If a problem arises, first look to the system for corrections and then communicate your solution to the person who can do something about it.
6. Be effective and efficient

    (Optimize every event...More with Less).

7. Have a willingness to win and allow others to win (Win/Win).
8. Focus on what works.
9. When in doubt, check feeling tone words.
10. Agree to agree.

Index

About the Author

Michael Reaves is the Southwest Regional Manager for Oreck Corporation and has utilized his creative talents in marketing and management for nearly twenty five years. He has served as a contract consultant to Continental Telephone, GTE, Mobil Oil and Amoco, and as a public speaker in business computer basics and company/employee interaction for productivity gains. Mr. Reaves has a solid background in business and is acutely aware of the importance of employee relations as he has held upper management positions of responsibility in national and international firms and formed his own firm.

Additional Titles in *The Entrepreneur's Guide Series* Available from Probus Publishing

How to Sell Your Business for the Best Price, Vaughn Cox

Entrepreneur's Guide to Capital, Revised Edition, Jennifer Lindsey

Cashflow, Credit and Collection, Basil P. Mavrovitis

Mastering the Business Cycle, Albert N. Link

Negotiating a Bank Loan, Arthur G. Pulis III

Crafting the Perfect Name, George Burroughs Blake and Nancy Blake-Bohné

Acquisitions, Sharon L. Blanding

Telemarketing That Works, Raymond C. Harlan and Walter M. Woolfson, Jr.

Building a Winning Sales Team, Gini Graham Scott

Employee Matters, E. Kenneth Snyder

Short-Term Money, Jeff Madura, E. Theodore Veit & Daniel E. McCarty

Forthcoming Title

How to Export, Roger Fritz, Available in March 1992